KU-066-303

EYEWITNESS
CAT

Jaguar

Abyssinian kittens

Tabby cat

Ocelot

Abyssinian

Puma cub

Ginger and white cat

Black leopard

Maine coon

 **CANADA WATER LIBRARY**
21 Surrey Quays Road
London SE16 7AR
Council

www.southwark.gov.uk/libraries @SouthwarkLibs

Please return/renew this item by
the last date shown.
Books may also be renewed by
phone and Internet.

SOUTHWARK LIBRARIES

SK 2836080 X

EYEWITNESS
CAT

WRITTEN BY
JULIET CLUTTON-BROCK

Serval

Russian blue

Tiger

Bobcat

REVISED EDITION
DK LONDON
Senior Editor Carron Brown
Art Editor Chrissy Barnard
Managing Editor Francesca Baines
Managing Art Editor Philip Letsu
Production Editor Kavita Varma
Production Controller Sian Cheung
Senior Jackets Designer Surabhi Wadhwa-Gandhi
Jacket Design Development Manager Sophia MTT
Publisher Andrew Macintyre
Associate Publishing Director Liz Wheeler
Art Director Karen Self
Publishing Director Jonathan Metcalf

Consultant Rae Foreman

DK DELHI
Senior Editor Shatarupa Chaudhuri
Senior Art Editor Vikas Chauhan
Project Art Editors Mansi Agrawal, Heena Sharma
Editor Sai Prasanna
Assistant Art Editor Aparajita Sen
Picture Researcher Vishal Ghavri
Managing Editor Kingshuk Ghoshal
Managing Art Editor Govind Mittal
DTP Designers Pawan Kumar, Rakesh Kumar,
Nandkishor Acharya
Jacket Designer Juhi Sheth

FIRST EDITION
Project Editor Gillian Denton
Art Editor Thomas Keenes
Senior Editor Helen Parker
Senior Art Editor Julia Harris
Production Louise Barratt
Picture Researcher Diana Morris
Special Photography Dave King
Additional Special Photography Philip Dowell,
Colin Keates ABIPP

This Eyewitness ® Book has been conceived by
Dorling Kindersley Limited and Editions Gallimard

This edition published in 2022
First published in Great Britain in 1991 by
Dorling Kindersley Limited
DK, One Embassy Gardens, 8 Viaduct Gardens,
London, SW11 7BW

The authorised representative in the EEA is
Dorling Kindersley Verlag GmbH. Arnulfstr. 124,
80636 Munich, Germany

Copyright © 1991, 2004, 2014, 2022
Dorling Kindersley Limited
A Penguin Random House Company
10 9 8 7 6 5 4 3 2 1
001-326775–Apr/2022

All rights reserved.
No part of this publication may be reproduced, stored in
or introduced into a retrieval system, or transmitted, in any
form, or by any means (electronic, mechanical, photocopying,
recording, or otherwise), without the prior written
permission of the copyright owner.

A CIP catalogue record for this book is
available from the British Library.
ISBN 978-0-2415-3628-5

Printed and bound in China

For the curious
www.dk.com

MIX
Paper from
responsible sources
FSC™ C018179

This book was made with Forest Stewardship Council™ certified
paper – one small step in DK's commitment to a sustainable future.
For more information go to www.dk.com/our-green-pledge

Early Greek gold
necklace plate

Puma

Lion

Contents

Leopard

What is a cat?

Good and evil
In Christian communities, cats have always represented both good and evil. Here, good and bad cat spirits fight over the soul of a cat woman.

Cats are possibly the most beautiful and graceful of all animals. They have fine fur, which is often strikingly marked with spots or stripes (p. 14), and elegant heads with pointed ears and large eyes. Wild and domestic cats all belong to one family, the Felidae. Cats have all the typical features of mammals: they are warm-blooded, have a protective skeleton, and produce milk to feed their young. All cats are carnivores, or meat eaters, and they almost all live and hunt on their own. Exceptions include lions, cheetahs, and certain domestic cats, which hunt in a family group, or pride. Affectionate, intelligent, and playful, the domestic cat is one of the most popular of all animal companions.

Now you see me...
This jaguar is well hidden. The striped and spotted fur of the cat family provides very effective camouflage in forests, jungles, grasslands, and plains.

Lindisfarne Gospels
The beautiful Lindisfarne Gospels – an illuminated copy of the four gospels – were written and decorated in Britain in around 700 CE. Domestic cats were clearly familiar animals at this time.

The stripes and markings of this domestic cat are inherited from its wild ancestor.

Adaptation
Domestic cats are very adaptable. They are found all over the world, from tropical Africa to icy Greenland. The domestic cat is the only member of the cat family that lives and breeds happily within human society.

Whiskers are organs of touch and help all cats – big, small, wild, or domestic – to feel objects in the dark.

Cats in Japan

The Japanese have a definite sympathy with the mysterious cat. In art, they have often shown its changeable nature by portraying one cat made up of many others.

All cats have claws and all except the cheetah sheathe them when at rest (pp. 42-43).

The mane of the adult male lion is the only obvious sign of sexual difference in the whole cat family.

Cooperative cats

Lions live and hunt with other members of their pride. Like all cats, lions kill their prey by stalking their victim, then leaping on it and biting into its neck (pp. 28-29).

The first cats

Stuck on you

In the Ice Age, an eruption of black, sticky tar at Rancho La Brea, now part of modern Los Angeles, USA, trapped thousands of animals, including 2,000 sabre-toothed *Smilodon*.

Millions of years ago, many cat-like animals roamed the Earth, some more massive and fierce than any alive today. The earliest fossil ancestors of the cat family come from the Eocene period, some 50 million years ago. These evolved into the species of large and small cats that are living today. There were also the now-extinct, sabre-toothed cats named after their enlarged, dagger-like canine teeth. The best known is the American species *Smilodon*.

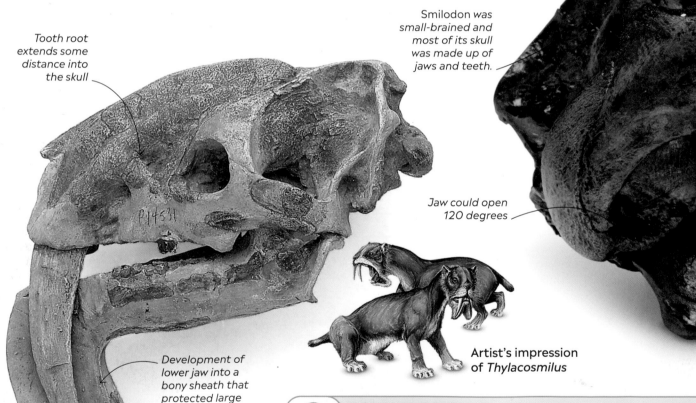

Smilodon was small-brained and most of its skull was made up of jaws and teeth.

Tooth root extends some distance into the skull

Jaw could open 120 degrees

Development of lower jaw into a bony sheath that protected large canine teeth

Continuously growing upper canine tooth

Artist's impression of *Thylacosmilus*

Thylacosmilus

Thylacosmilus looked like a sabre-toothed cat, but was not part of the cat family. It was a mammal that lived in South America during the Pliocene era about five million years ago.

👁 EYEWITNESS

Digging up bones

Prehistoric archaeologist Jordi Serangeli has been leading a large-scale excavation in an ancient site at Schöningen, Germany. He discovered several fossils of sabre-toothed cats, including the rare European species *Homotherium latidens*. Here, he is seen holding a fossilized bone of a 300,000–year–old sabre-toothed tiger.

Smilodon

This large, sabre-toothed cat lived on open grasslands in family groups and preyed on large herd animals. *Smilodon* became extinct about 14,000 years ago.

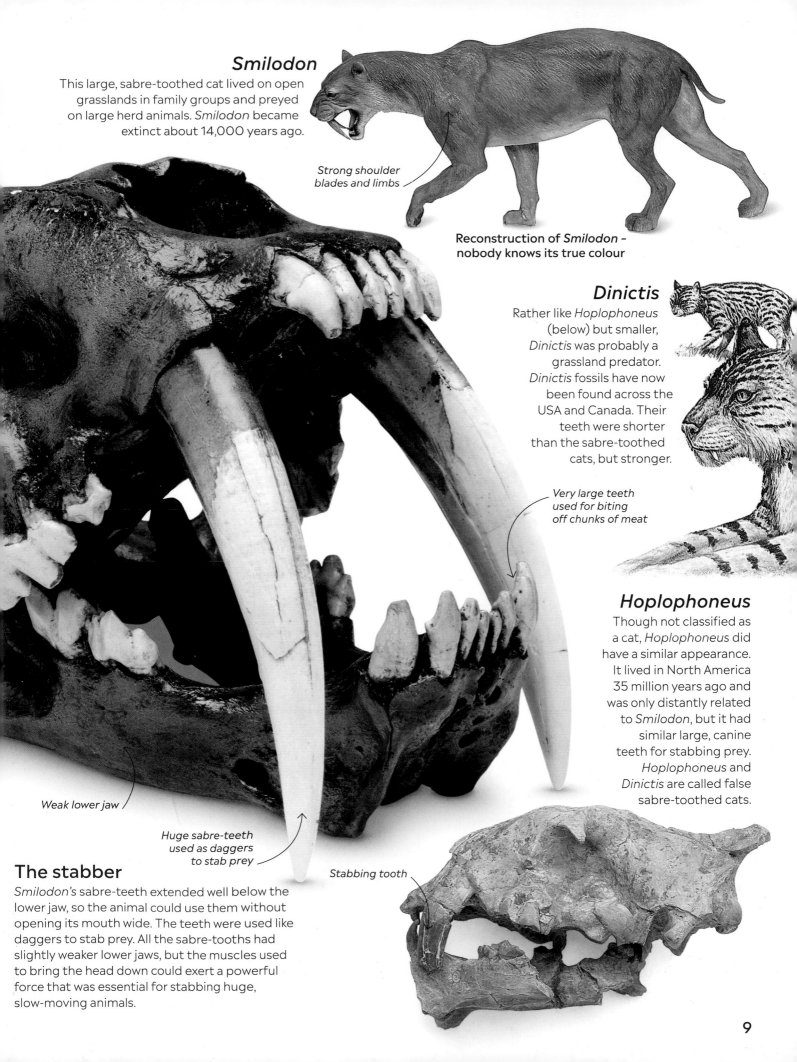

Strong shoulder blades and limbs

Reconstruction of *Smilodon* – nobody knows its true colour

Dinictis

Rather like *Hoplophoneus* (below) but smaller, *Dinictis* was probably a grassland predator. *Dinictis* fossils have now been found across the USA and Canada. Their teeth were shorter than the sabre-toothed cats, but stronger.

Very large teeth used for biting off chunks of meat

Hoplophoneus

Though not classified as a cat, *Hoplophoneus* did have a similar appearance. It lived in North America 35 million years ago and was only distantly related to *Smilodon*, but it had similar large, canine teeth for stabbing prey. *Hoplophoneus* and *Dinictis* are called false sabre-toothed cats.

Weak lower jaw

Huge sabre-teeth used as daggers to stab prey

Stabbing tooth

The stabber

Smilodon's sabre-teeth extended well below the lower jaw, so the animal could use them without opening its mouth wide. The teeth were used like daggers to stab prey. All the sabre-tooths had slightly weaker lower jaws, but the muscles used to bring the head down could exert a powerful force that was essential for stabbing huge, slow-moving animals.

9

Cat clans

Cats kill other animals for food and so belong to the order Carnivora (flesh eaters). Wildcats are comprised of two species – the European wildcat, *Felis silvestris*, and the African wildcat, *Felis lybica*. The domestic cat, *Felis catus*, is descended from the African wildcat. Members of the two wildcat species can be found throughout much of the world, including Scotland, Germany, Turkey, Africa, central Asia, the Middle East, and China. Cats have well-developed senses, fast movements, and very sharp teeth. Unlike the large cats, the small cats are unable to roar.

👁 **EYEWITNESS**

Naming cats
German naturalist Johann von Schreber (1739–1810) coined the scientific name *Felis silvestris*. He followed the system of giving Latin names to species, invented by Swedish botanist Carl von Linné. Schreber also named other cat species, such as the caracal and jungle cat.

Pumas have slender bodies like house cats.

Puma
The puma, or cougar, is an oversized small cat that can purr like a domestic cat. It lives in North and South America.

Bobcat
The bobcat is the most common wildcat in North America. It looks rather like a lynx without the long ear tufts.

Domestic cat
There are almost as many breeds of domestic cats as there are of dogs.

Small cats

All the small cats (including the smaller wildcats) live on their own and hunt by night. They are found all over the world, and, tragically, many have been hunted almost to extinction for their beautifully patterned, soft furs.

Weighs between 109 and 226 kg (240 and 500 lb)

Big cats

The big cats need a great deal of meat to survive. This means they have always been fewer in number than the small cats, who are more able to find enough food for their needs.

Tiger

The tiger is the largest and heaviest of all the cats. It is a night hunter, and preys on animals smaller than itself. Tigers are found from tropical India to icy Siberia.

Odd cats out

The clouded leopard does not roar like the other big cats, nor does it groom or rest like a small cat. The cheetah is unique because it is a running cat (pp. 42–43), whereas all others are leaping cats.

Clouded leopard

The clouded leopard lives in the forests of Southeast Asia, but it is rarely seen and is in danger of extinction.

Cheetah

Cheetahs do not have sheaths over their claws and can run at great speed. This has helped them to adapt to life on the grasslands of Africa where many animals compete for food.

THE DESCENT OF THE CAT

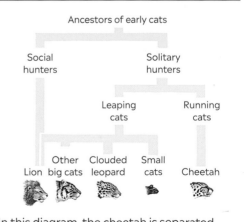

Ancestors of early cats

Social hunters

Solitary hunters

Leaping cats

Running cats

Lion

Other big cats

Clouded leopard

Small cats

Cheetah

In this diagram, the cheetah is separated from all the other cats because it is the only one able to chase its prey at great speed. However, like other cats, it still kills its prey by leaping on it and biting its neck. All other cats are called leaping cats, because they slowly stalk their prey and then leap on it.

The bare bones

A cat's skeleton consists of about 250 bones. It protects the soft parts of the body, while allowing the cat to move with great agility. The skull is specially designed for killing prey. The eye sockets are round to allow a wide field of vision, the hearing parts are large, and the short, strong jaws open very wide. Cats kill their prey with their very sharp canine teeth and then cut pieces off with their carnassial (shearing) teeth.

Night prowler
This snow leopard reveals its fearsome teeth before it attacks.

Canine tooth

Large eye socket

High crest for attachment of jaw muscles

Spine of thoracic vertebrae

Neck vertebrae

Very heavy lower jaw for powerful bite

Shoulder bone (scapula)

Muscles
In order to pounce on prey, climb trees, run fast, and groom every part of its body, the cat has to be amazingly supple. The muscle connections between the bones of the neck and the back allow the cat to stretch in all directions.

Big and small cats stretch in exactly the same way

Thoracic rib

Breast bone (sternum)

Elbow joint

Front leg bone (ulna)

Front leg bone (radius)

Cat skeleton
Although the domestic cat and tiger have similar, skeletons, the small cat has a different larynx enabling it to purr, the sheaths of its claws are longer, and its tail is more flexible.

Wrist (carpal) bones

Claws in their sheaths

Cat skulls

This skull shows the big, round eye sockets of the domestic cat, its short face, and large, sharp teeth. In some breeds of domestic cat, such as the Persians, the face has been bred to be so short that there is hardly any room for the teeth.

Eye socket (orbit)

Front view of domestic cat skull

Biting tooth (incisor)

Side view of domestic cat skull

Killing tooth (canine)

Cutting tooth (carnassial)

Tiger skeleton

Lumbar vertebrae

Four false ribs are not attached to the sternum

Costal cartilages join the ribs to the sternum

Sacral vertebrae

Hip bone (pelvis)

Thigh bone (femur)

Hip joint

Just a bite

All cats can open their mouths very wide. This is due to the thick bones at the angle of the jaw, and the powerful ligaments that join the lower jaw to the upper jaw.

Knee cap (patella)

Caudal vertebrae

Tiger skeleton

Cats have rounded skulls with short jaws. The seven neck vertebrae are shorter than in most mammals, and the brain case (cranium) is large. The ribcage is deep and the powerful hind leg bones are longer than the foreleg bones. The number of tail bones varies from species to species.

Knee joint

Back leg bone (fibula)

The skeleton shows that with so few tail vertebrae this Manx cat would have had no visible tail.

Missing link

The Manx cat has been known on the Isle of Man for at least 200 years (p. 59). Its very short tail is thought to be a result of inbreeding (breeding within closely related animals).

Back leg bone (tibia)

Toeing the line

It is impossible for a person to stand on tiptoe without support; ballet dancers wear special blocks to do this. The bones and joints in cats' feet have evolved to allow them to always walk on their toes.

Heel bone (calcaneum)

Hind foot (tarsal) bones

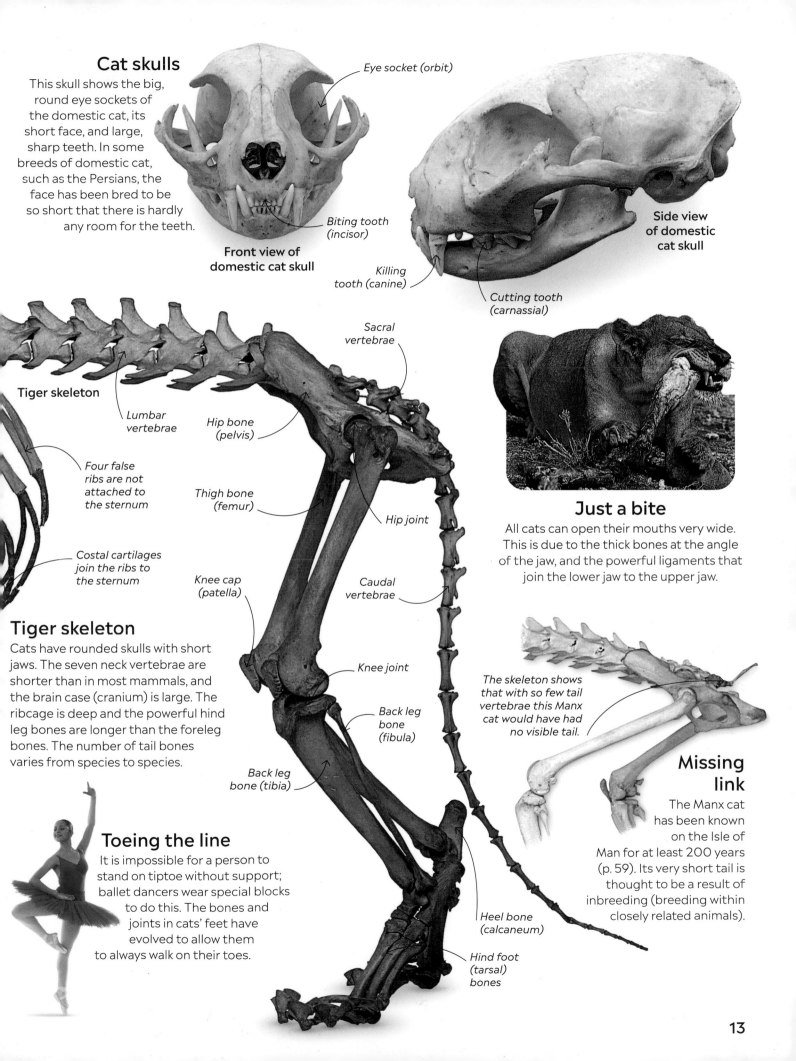

13

Inside **out**

Cats have evolved so that they can feed on other live animals. They have to be fast thinkers, fast killers, and, in order to outwit other predators, fast eaters. Their intestines are relatively short and simple because they need to digest only meat and not plant matter. Compared to wildcats who may gorge on large prey, domestic cats who hunt their own food may feed up to 20 times a day on small prey. Cats are very intelligent and their brains are large in relation to the size of their bodies. Small cats communicate with each other by purring. Coats of the big cats can help camouflage them so they can hide and hunt better.

Gene machine

The curly coat of this rex is an abnormality caused by inbreeding (p. 13). Inbreeding can lead to genetic changes in the offspring.

Time for a drink

A puma drinks from a freshwater pool. All cats except the sand cat (p. 39) need water regularly.

Rounded head with short face

Lithe body

Whiskers

Long legs

Fur

A cat's fur keeps the animal warm, acts as camouflage, carries the animal's scent, and is sensitive to touch (pp. 16–17). All wildcats have an undercoat of fine, soft wool, covered by an outer coat of coarser, longer hairs (guard hairs). These outer hairs carry the coat's spotted or striped pattern.

Spot me

The spotted coat of this leopard provides perfect camouflage in the sun-dappled, wooded grasslands. Only its tawny-yellow eyes can be seen, waiting for any movement that might mean food.

Fur coats

The furs on the right have very different patterns. For hundreds of years people have used animal furs to make coats. Today, people realize that it is cruel to kill animals for their furs.

Tiger

Ocelot

Jaguar

Serval

Leopard

CLAWS FOR CONCERN

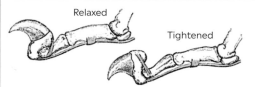

Relaxed

Tightened

All cats except for cheetahs have sheathed claws. When the claws are relaxed, they are covered by a bony sheath (top). Special muscles extend the claws, and the toes spread out at the same time.

Claws

A cat's claws are made of keratin, a protein also found in human nails. The hind paws have four claws; the fore paws have five. The fifth claw helps the cat to grip when climbing or holding prey.

Naughty puss
This American illustration shows how a playful cat can inflict painful scratches.

Purrfect communication

In the small cats, the set of bones at the base of the tongue is hard and bony, which allows them to purr. The sound is made when these bones vibrate. A cat usually purrs when it is relaxed and content.

CAT'S DIGESTIVE SYSTEM

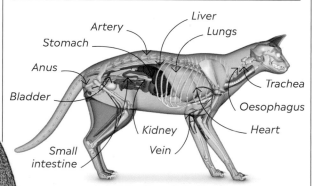

Artery — Liver — Lungs

Stomach

Anus

Bladder

Trachea

Oesophagus

Heart

Kidney — Vein

Small intestine

A cat's food passes from the throat to the stomach via a passage called the oesophagus. It then goes to the small intestine, where the nutrients are absorbed into the bloodstream. Waste passes through the large intestine and out of the anus.

Long tail for balance

Good points

The muscular body of the lioness has a rounded head, a short face, and rather long legs. The long tail helps the heavy cat to balance when she makes rapid changes of direction while chasing prey. Sensitive whiskers on the sides of her face help her to find her way around in the dark. The senses of sight, smell, hearing, and balance are particularly well developed in all cats, both big and small.

Muscles

The muscles in the cat's shoulders are very powerful and are used when the animal leaps onto its prey.

Supersenses

Most wildcats hunt at night. They have highly developed senses so that they can move quietly, see everything around them, hear the slightest noise, and smell any other animals in the dark. The small cat has to be alert, ready to flee if threatened. Cats have one sense that humans do not have, known as the "taste-smell" sense. Cats have a legendary homing instinct and there are many stories of cats finding their way home over long distances.

Mind the gap
Cats use their highly sensitive whiskers and guard (outer) hairs to judge distances. So if there is room for the fur, there is room for the cat's body.

Flehmen
By curling back his upper lip in a special grimace (flehmen), the lion is using the Jacobson's (taste-smell) organ to tell if there is a lioness ready to mate nearby.

 EYEWITNESS

Cell mates
In 1601, the Earl of Southampton was imprisoned in the Tower of London for rebelling against Elizabeth I. The story goes that his cat found its way alone across the city to the Tower. Once there, he crossed roofs until he found the room where the Earl was being held and climbed down the chimney. The story may well be true, because this portrait was painted at the time.

The eyes have it
Cats have a layer of extra reflecting cells in their eyes called the *tapetum lucidum* (p. 64). These reflectors help them see in the dark. They shine if the eyes are caught in headlights.

Pupils expanded (above), narrowed (below)

Pupil power
A cat's eyes are quite round and can look in a wide angle all around the head. In darkness, the pupils expand widely to let in as much light as possible. In bright light, they narrow to tiny slits in small cats, or to tight circles in big cats.

Stretch 'n' sniff
When cats are presented with food or any strange object, they are always cautious. They may first reach out and tap it with a paw, before stretching out and exploring it with their nose.

Tortoiseshell and white cat

Cats' sense of smell helps them recognize food, objects, other animals, and humans

Five senses

In all cats, the senses of sight, hearing, smell, taste, and touch are more highly developed than in humans. Although humans are more sensitive to colour, cats have superior vision in low light conditions compared to humans. They can also navigate better through other senses.

Large, funnel-shaped ears draw sound waves into the inner ear, so that the cat can judge the direction of a noise

Eyes open wide when a cat is alert and interested and close to a slit when it is angry and frightened

Whiskers

Whiskers are long, stiff hairs with sensitive nerve endings at their roots. They spread out round the face of the cat so that it can feel where it is in relation to objects nearby. In bad light, they act as a backup to the cat's sight.

Nose, which has no covering, is very sensitive and draws in scents to receptors on many thin, curled bones in the front of the skull

Rough tongue used for grooming the coat, cleaning kittens, and lapping up liquids (pp. 20–21). Sense of taste is important, because as the cat bolts its meat, it must be able to distinguish quickly any part that might be rotten and harmful

Sorrel Abyssinian

Magnificent movers

All cats are extremely agile and can leap with great power, although, apart from the cheetah, they can run fast over only short distances (pp. 42–43). Unlike many other carnivores, the cat has collar bones, which prevent it from jarring its shoulders when it leaps from a height. The shoulder blades are placed well at the sides of the cat's chest, which helps it to climb. Cats that spend a lot of time in trees, such as the leopard (pp. 32–33), have long tails for balance. All cats walk on their toes and their feet have thick, soft pads so they can move quietly.

Cat is at full stretch in mid-leap

Cat puts all four paws together for maximum power at take-off

One giant leap...
Cats jump by flexing and relaxing the muscles of the limbs and back, while balancing with the tail. Unlike many other jumping animals, a cat can judge its landing position with great accuracy. This is essential for a hunter of fast-moving, small prey.

Puma cub

Cat balances on back paws as it begins leap

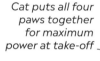

Nine lives
Cats can fall from great heights and always seem to land on their feet. Many of the small cats, as well as the leopard, spend much of their lives in trees. Their highly developed sense of balance helps them hunt fast-moving animals like squirrels, while creeping along a flimsy branch. The nervous system has evolved so that the cat can right itself mid-flight to avoid damaging its body on landing.

When running slowly, opposite legs go together – right foreleg and left hind leg move in unison

Practice
All cubs and kittens have to exercise their limbs and muscles before they can be as flexible as their parents. This young cub's paws seem too big for its body, but with practice it will soon be as agile as its mother.

RUNNING WILD

When a cat runs, it pushes off with both back legs at the same time, but places the front paws down separately. English photographer Eadweard Muybridge (1830–1904) took this famous sequence in 1887 to show how a cat moves when running.

Front paws land and cat begins to bring back paws forwards

All four paws touch land

Tail is essential for balance, like the pole carried by a tightrope walker

Cool cat

Few cats seem to enjoy swimming, apart from tigers and jaguars, who spend time in or near water. Tigers living in the tropical rainforests of Asia use the water to keep cool.

Balancing act

This cat shows how it can walk along the top of a very high, very narrow fence. It places its paws neatly one in front of the other and is never in danger of falling.

Loose skin, and muscles not yet developed

Sitting on a tree

Small and big cats have to learn to climb. At first, they often venture too far up a tree and are then terrified of going up or down. After a few false starts, however, most of them land on their feet. Leopards are skilled climbers.

19

Cleaning **up**

Cats are exceptionally clean animals. They spend a lot of time licking their fur, pulling dirt from their feet, and wiping their faces with their paws. Grooming allows the cat to spread its scent all over its body and then to rub it onto people, objects, and other animals. It also helps the cat to relax. Domestic cats usually bury their droppings, unlike many wildcats who deposit them in prominent positions to mark their territory (pp. 26–27). Licking, rubbing, and depositing droppings are all part of a cat's complex pattern of communication through smell and touch.

Most cats do not like water, but these kittens by cat artist Louis Wain (1860–1939) seem to be having fun.

Flexibility of neck allows cat to reach all parts of the body

Papillae, each shaped like a miniature tongue

Tongue tool

The cat's tongue contains hard, spiny points called papillae, which are used to scrape meat off bones, or to lick up food and push it down the throat. The tongue can also be used as a scoop to lap up water, or as a comb to groom the fur.

Belly brush up

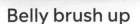

The cat licks its body to groom its fur and to strengthen its own scent after it has been stroked or has fed its kittens.

Litter box

Domestic cats can urinate and excrete in an indoor litter box, which makes it easy for owners to clean and refill. Cats sometimes mark their territory with unburied droppings, a behaviour called middening.

Cat litter commonly contains absorbent materials such as clay or silica gel.

Paw thoroughly dampened for washing face

Face flannel

The cat licks its paw, then rubs its foot round its jaws. This spreads its scent from glands in the chin to its feet, so its scent will be left wherever it walks.

Paws for action

If a cat walks on something sticky, it will wash it off at once. Clean paws are essential for fast movement and climbing – but washing the paws also helps to spread the cat's scent.

The rough tongue wets the paw in order to wash the face.

Cats lick their fur to remove odour and dirt.

Paws spread to give tongue maximum access

Reaching the parts...

In many cat species, including domestic cats and lions, females communally care for kittens and cubs. This care includes nursing and grooming. Grooming ensures cleanliness, can help aid digestion and toileting in young kittens, and spreads a communal scent over one another. The young learn to groom themselves by watching their mothers.

Personal hygiene

By grooming the inside of its leg, the cat is spreading scent from its chin and genital glands around its body.

Hunting

In the wild, all cats feed on the animals they have killed. Cats are solitary hunters, except for lions and cheetahs, which hunt in groups. Cats usually kill animals smaller than themselves, although sometimes they will attack a larger animal. Motionless animals might escape attack, but with practice, cats can recognize prey by sound and scent alone. Cats stalk their prey, then leap on it and bite into the neck. Small cats feed mostly on mice, birds, and other small animals. Large cats, like the leopard, feed on bigger animals about the size of a goat, and often drag their prey up into trees to keep it away from other predators.

A stalking cat holds its body close to the ground.

Tom and Jerry

In the famous cartoon, the cunning mouse Jerry often outwits the cat Tom – not often the case in real life.

The pads on a cat's paws help it to move silently.

Ready for action

This black leopard (also known as a panther) is stalking and getting ready for the kill. Every part of its body is on alert. All cats on the prowl move very slowly and silently until they are near enough to make a quick and decisive pounce.

Medieval mousers

This medieval picture comes from a 13th-century book called *The Harleian Bestiary*. It is interesting because it is a very early illustration of cats with a rat.

Wildcat leaping in the air after prey

In for the kill

Cats often choose a spot where they can see their prey without being seen. This cat would have been sitting absolutely still on the fence for some time, before leaping down on the unsuspecting prey.

Black panther

The dark coat camouflages the animal at night.

A fishy business

The fishing cat of India can flip fish out of the water with its slightly webbed paws and has even been seen diving for fish.

A cat lashes its tail when angry and twitches it gently to and fro when concentrating or contented.

Running down

The cheetah will not begin to hunt unless there is an antelope on its own. The antelopes know this and will not be disturbed unless the cheetah comes too close. However, once the prey has been singled out, the cheetah will chase it at great speed.

A practised killer

Many cats play with their prey before killing it. Mother cats often show their kittens how to hunt by capturing prey and then releasing it. Some cats keep this kittenish behaviour in adult life. Domestic cats are fed but instinct drives them to play with toys they can hunt.

A cat playing with a toy is reacting as if it were prey.

Serval

Chicken dinner

Small cats, like this serval, crouch down to eat their food. They begin by eating the head, which is swallowed whole with very little chewing. Big cats tend to eat lying down.

Big meal

With its massive teeth, this tiger can snap a bone with one bite.

The young ones

The young of the large cats are usually called cubs, while the young of the small cats are called kittens. All cats are blind until they are at least nine days old. Domestic cats will choose a safe, dark spot like a drawer or cupboard to give birth, and there are usually about four kittens in a litter. Kittens take around 63 days to develop in the mother's womb (gestate), and after birth, the mother gives them milk for six to eight weeks before they are weaned and begin to eat meat. In the wild, most cats give birth in a den. Lion cubs take between 100 and 119 days to gestate and they are not weaned until they are three months old.

Knitting kitten
The kitten in this Japanese scroll is playing with a ball of wool. Playing with toys helps kittens to learn how to catch and hunt.

Lion king
When a lioness is on heat (ready to mate), the chief lion in a pride stays close to her and prevents other lions approaching. They mate many times over two or three days.

Family gathering
Although domestic cats may live in a town flat and have no contact with life in the wild, they still have all the instincts of wildcats. These kittens are now weaned, but the mother continues to protect and groom them. She also teaches them how to clean themselves and where to bury their waste.

Moggies mating
A female cat allows a male to mate with her only when she is on heat. In domestic cats, this usually happens twice a year. While on heat, the female may mate several times with different males (p. 61).

Kitten grows adult coat of fine hairs over woolly undercoat

Playing about

Play is an essential part of growing up. These kittens have to learn how to fight, but they must learn when to stop as well, so they are not hurt. Play also exercises the muscles of young animals and helps the brain to develop quick reactions.

Identity crisis

Cubs and kittens often have differently marked coats from the adults. This spotty baby is, in fact, a puma. Its spots and stripes slowly fade as it grows up. Siamese kittens are born pale all over. The dark points develop only as the cat becomes an adult.

Sorrel Abyssinian cat and kittens

Mother's rough tongue grooms kitten, helping it to understand about other cats' scents

Legs slightly bandy and uncertain at first

Cub carriage

All mother cats are expert at carrying their young at the first hint of danger. This lioness grasps the loose skin around the neck of her cub between her teeth and carries it without hurting it at all.

Several pairs of teats for suckling – each kitten has its own teat and uses no other

Cat traits

Throughout domestication, cats have adjusted to living with humans, but have retained many of the behaviours of their ancestors. Wild and domesticated cats behave in very similar ways. They give birth in safe, dark places, they exchange scents, and they hunt alone (apart from the lion). They also all mark their territory by spraying urine and by depositing their droppings. Both large and small cats have various noises in common, such as chirruping a greeting and yowling. All cats sleep a great deal, mostly in the day, so that they are ready for hunting at night.

Lion lingo
The roar of the lion is one of the most frightening of all animal sounds. However, the lion roars as a means of communicating with the rest of the pride, rather than to frighten its prey.

Cat nap
Cats sleep a great deal. In hot countries, they may sleep up to 18 hours a day, hunting and feeding in the cooler hours. Cats usually sleep in several shortish periods, often with one eye partly open.

Flattened ears are a warning sign

Hissing indicates that this cat does not want to be interfered with

Tail curved around the body and tucked in

Friend...
Cats value their personal space. This cat feels that the other cat has come too close so she has crouched down in a defensive position.

Putting our heads together
Cats that live together, like domestic cats or lions, sometimes rub each other's heads to show that they have no intention of fighting.

Leaving a message

All cats mark their territory with urine and fluid from their glands. This is called spraying and they all do it in the same way. The cat backs up to a post or tree, lifts its rump high, and, with the tail held straight up, discharges a stream of strong-smelling fluid against the object.

Smartening up

Cats spend a good deal of their time "sharpening their claws". This is really stretching their limbs by digging their claws into a wooden tree (or silk-covered sofa!) and pulling the claws downwards. The claws are cleaned, and the muscles of the feet and limbs are exercised. Scratching also acts as a visual mark to other cats that there are cats in the area or that the territory is claimed.

Back slightly arched to make cat look bigger

Lioness scratching

Lions can tear the bark off a tree when "sharpening their claws".

Twitching tail shows that the cat is in an excited state

...Or foe?

Cats test each other's reactions with an explorative paw. As this cat is getting a negative reaction from the tortoiseshell cat, he will probably just stalk off. To avoid injury, domestic cats would rather hiss, crouch, and retreat than fight.

Roly poly

All cats roll over on their backs to show affection or to show that a female is on heat (p. 24). They expose their bellies in this way only when they feel secure.

Leggings

Cats often rub against people's legs to show affection and to transfer their scent.

In a pride

More than 10,000 years ago, lions roamed the whole of Europe, Asia, and Africa. Apart from a small number in northwest India, lions today are found only in Africa. They live in family groups, or prides, of up to 12 animals. As they hunt together, they are able to kill animals larger than themselves. Male lions defend their territory by pacing around it, roaring, and spraying their urine. The females are the main hunters. Each lioness will give birth to about five cubs every two years. If a new lion takes over a pride, he may kill any cubs a lioness has before he mates with her.

Star sign of Leo

People born under Leo are said to be proud, brave, and strong, just like the lion itself.

The king and his mates

His magnificent mane, heavy body, and huge canine teeth ensure that the lion rules his world. Males are always allowed to feed first at a kill. The lionesses are the core of any pride, and stick close to their female relatives. They have strong, lithe bodies and creep stealthily before moving in for the kill.

The pride

Females always outnumber males in a pride. When a young male reaches adulthood, the resident male usually drives him away. He will then join a group of females in need of a male. The male's main role is to defend the pride's territory.

A lion can go without water for a few days but needs to eat
7 kg (16 lb)
of meat a day.

Herakles

In Greek myth, Herakles had to perform 12 tasks. The first was to kill the Nemean lion whose skin could not be pierced – so he choked it to death.

Strong and powerful paws help lions catch and hold their prey

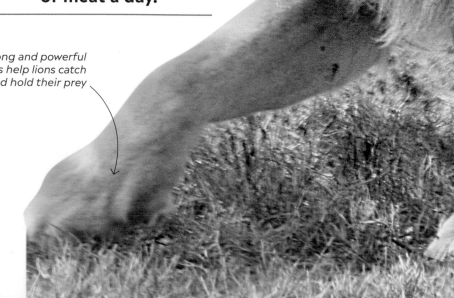

Iranian plate

This plate shows a lion with the Sun rising behind him. This was the symbol of Iranian kingship.

 EYEWITNESS

Tamed lioness

Naturalist Joy Adamson (1910–1980) and her husband George raised a lion cub they named Elsa. When Elsa grew up, they decided to train her to hunt and release her into the wild. Joy (seen here) wrote about her experiences in her book *Born Free* (1960).

African lion and lioness

The mane makes the lion look bigger than he really is. It may help to frighten off other lions.

Having no mane helps the lioness to hunt

The tiger

Tigers are the biggest and most powerful cats. They used to live in the forests of India, southeast Asia, and China. Today, these endangered creatures live in a few tropical forest reserves and in swamps, like the Ganges Delta in India. The largest tigers come from the icy forests of Siberia, but only between 400 and 500 still live there. Their habitat has been slowly destroyed and they have been poached for their skins and bones. Tigers hunt and defend their territories on their own. Though cats generally avoid water, tigers are strong swimmers and spend a good deal of time keeping cool in or near rivers. They often hide the carcasses of their prey in dense thickets or in water.

Storm tiger
In this painting by French artist Henri Rousseau (1844–1910), the tiger is well camouflaged.

Pattern of stripes is not same on both sides

Bachhus is shown on a tiger as Romans believed that he had conquered India.

Tiger ride
A mosaic pavement, dating from the first to 2nd century CE was discovered in London, England. It shows Bacchus, the Roman god of wine, calmly riding a tiger.

Very long, closely striped tail

Heavy body is close to the ground so the tiger can be hidden in grass or water

Heavy beast
The lion may be called the king of the beasts because of its great mane and proud carriage, but the tiger is more awesome. Tigers in India weigh up to 260 kg (573 lb) and the Siberian tiger is even heavier. Yet, despite their size, tigers live and hunt in the same way as all other cats.

EYEWITNESS

Tiger expert
Conservationist Ullas Karanth pioneered the use of camera traps to estimate tiger populations in forests. He founded the Centre for Wildlife Studies in India. His research has helped protect Bengal tigers. Writer R K Narayan consulted Karanth for his book *A Tiger for Malgudi* (1983).

Tiger by a torrent

This scroll, painted by Japanese artist Kishi Ganku (1756–1838), shows a fierce tiger beside a raging torrent.

The artist used ink and colour on silk.

A sharp sense of hearing helps in hunting.

Mass murder

In India, the tiger was always respected until the mid-19th century, when the British took power. During this time, huge numbers of tigers were killed at shooting parties. Today, the tiger is again respected, and the Indian government has set up Project Tiger to save it from extinction.

Killer tigers

Tigers do not usually kill humans, although it can happen. It may be because they are injured and can no longer kill wild animals. Or it may be that people working in their territories have scared off their natural prey. In India, the government is doing all it can to keep people and tigers apart.

The huge paw is so powerful, that it can knock prey over with one blow.

Tippu's tiger
This large mechanical "toy" was made during the Mughal Empire (1526–1857) in India. When the handle is turned, the tiger attacks the English soldier.

Tree climber

Leopards live in the wooded grasslands of Africa and southern Asia. Although bulky, they are skilled climbers and can scale vertical trunks with complete ease. Leopards are secretive animals and stealthy hunters. They may occasionally prey on domestic farm animals, but they also kill animals, such as baboons and cane rats that destroy crops. Cubs are looked after by the mother until they are about two years old. Leopards are under threat everywhere, mainly because of the destruction of their habitat, but also because they have very desirable fur.

The Journey of the Magi
This painting by Gozzoli was commissioned by Piero de Medici for the chapel of his family palace in Florence, Italy. The Medicis kept leopards for hunting.

Benin bronze

This bronze plaque was made in the Bini kingdom in Nigeria in the 16th or 17th century. Known as the King of the Bush, the leopard was an important animal in Benin folklore. It was chosen as the king of the animals for its power, beauty, good nature, and wisdom.

Leopards do not often roar but communicate by means of a rasping bark.

The coat is short and sleek in countries where the climate is hot, but becomes much thicker and warmer in colder climate.

Leopard

The black spots on a tawny-yellow background act as a perfect camouflage for this shy animal as it hides in the dappled leaves of a tree or in the long, dry grass. Leopards often carry their prey into trees. This protects the carcasses from hyenas and jackals, which would soon scrounge the food from the solitary leopard, if it were left on the ground.

Spotless

The black panther is any large cat – usually a leopard or a jaguar – with hidden spots. Its colour comes from the combination of its genes. The panther behaves just like spotted leopards and breeds freely with them.

Panther
You can just see the spots on this panther's coat. This type of coat is most common in southeast Asia.

Spots or rosette patterns are visible up close

Bagheera
Bagheera, the black panther, played an important part in Rudyard Kipling's *The Jungle Book.*

Snow leopard

This very rare, large cat is not the same species as the true leopard. A solitary hunter, it lives only in the high mountains of central Asia.

The leopard's tail is long and darkly ringed.

The soft-looking paw hides sharp claws used for killing prey and climbing trees.

Water cat

The jaguar is the only large cat to be found in the Americas. It lives mainly in the tropical forests of South America, and it, until quite recently, was also fairly common in the southern states of the USA. However, although it is now protected, the jaguar is in real danger of extinction due to the destruction of its forest habitat and hunting. The jaguar is larger than a leopard, but not as agile. A solitary hunter, it kills tapirs, turtles, and other small animals. It can climb trees, but prefers to hunt on the ground or in water.

Tiahuanaco tapestry
This Peruvian tapestry, made approximately 1,000 years ago, illustrates the importance of the jaguar in Peruvian society. It shows a full-face jaguar head, flanked by two standing jaguars.

Tapir trapper
Tapirs were once an important part of the jaguar's diet. They live in the Amazonian forests, but tapirs are very scarce today.

Spotted head held low

Long tail helps the jaguar to balance

The heavy body of the jaguar is a bit like a lion's.

Reddish-coloured spots. Forest jaguars are darker than those living in grasslands.

Grunter hunter
The jaguar is not as bold as the leopard, and is generally slower. Unlike most big cats, it rarely roars. It grunts frequently when hunting and growls when threatened.

Aquacat

Jaguars swim well and have been known to kill crocodiles. The Amazon peoples believe that jaguars lure fish to the surface by twitching their tails in the water. They then flip the fish out with their paws. River turtles are also a favourite food.

This jaguar at the Zoo de Bordeaux-Pessac, France, has caught a fish.

Peruvian pot

Jaguars often featured in South American myths. This pot from Peru shows a jaguar eating its victim.

👁 EYEWITNESS

Protecting jaguars

Renowned wildcat scientist Dr Alan Rabinowitz (1953–2018) established the world's first jaguar sanctuary, the Cockscomb Basin Wildlife Sanctuary, in Belize. As a child, he had made a promise to a jaguar at a zoo that he would protect this species and other cats as well. He tells his story in his children's book *A Boy and A Jaguar* (2014).

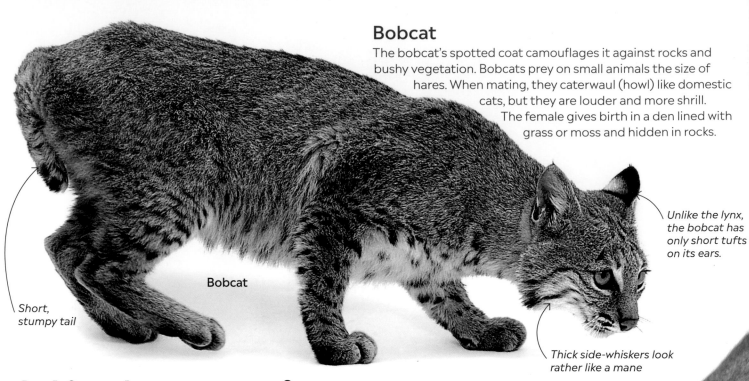

Bobcat

The bobcat's spotted coat camouflages it against rocks and bushy vegetation. Bobcats prey on small animals the size of hares. When mating, they caterwaul (howl) like domestic cats, but they are louder and more shrill. The female gives birth in a den lined with grass or moss and hidden in rocks.

Bobcat

Unlike the lynx, the bobcat has only short tufts on its ears.

Short, stumpy tail

Thick side-whiskers look rather like a mane

High society

Pupils are circular, and do not contract to slits as in the smaller cats

Trapped

Hunting for bobcat and lynx is still allowed in North America, and thousands of bobcats are caught for their fur every year, often in vicious traps like this.

The lynx, bobcat, and puma or cougar, are called small cats, although they are not that small. The puma is the largest of all the small cats. The lynx and the bobcat are different from other cats in that they both have very short tails. The bobcat lives in North America, the lynx in Europe, North America, and Asia, and the puma in North and South America. All three are most at home high up on rocky mountain slopes.

Puma

The puma is as much at home on the windswept shores of South America, as on the Colorado mountains in the western USA. It hides in rocky places and is a good climber. Pumas have large territories and cover long distances in search for prey. This captive puma is ready to pounce.

Change of scene

Although often found on mountains, pumas can also live in tropical rainforests.

Lynx in summer coat

Lynx in winter coat

Lynx

The lynx is best adapted to life in high pine forests and thick scrub where its brownish coat is invisible against moss and rocks. The long tufts on its ears are thought to help the lynx to hear well in dense forests. In winter, its big feet are covered with thick fur that acts like a snowshoe.

Sacred cat

In the Mochica culture of Peru around 600 BCE, the puma was worshipped as a god.

Coat can vary in colour, but the underside is always pale

Long, furry tail with a black tip, unlike the bobcat and the lynx

Hind legs are longer than the forelegs making the puma a good stalker

👁 EYEWITNESS

Puma project

Field biologists at the Santa Cruz Puma Project in the USA study the behaviour, physiology (body functions), and habitat of pumas. They fit pumas with tracking collars to collect data on their movement and location. The information is shared with other organizations to help conservation efforts.

Plains cats

Many cats live in grasslands (savanna), plains, and deserts. Plains cats hunt small animals, including birds, rodents, and snakes. They have longer legs than forest cats and are fairly speedy over short distances when escaping from larger predators, such as hyenas. The caracal is also called the desert lynx because it has tufts on its ears, although it does not have the short tail of the northern lynx. The serval has been hunted in East Africa for its meat and fur, which is used to make African cloaks called carosses.

Black ears with tufts of hair about 4.5 cm (1¾ in) long

Caracal

Caracal is a Turkish word meaning "black ears". The caracal is found in Africa, India, and western Asia. The female usually gives birth to two or three kittens in rock holes, borrowed burrows, or thick scrub. It has a loud bark, which it uses to call its mate.

Bird basher

In India and Persia (now Iran), the caracal, which is easily tamed, was trained to catch hares and birds. It is an excellent bird catcher, and sometimes leaps high into the air to knock down birds with its paw. Caracals climb well, and have been known to lunge at big birds and even kill eagles roosting in trees.

Caracal sprinting and catching a young ostrich

In up to the neck

The caracal lives in tall grasslands, dry scrub, and semi-desert.

Long, strong legs allow bursts of speed

Broad head with low-set ears

Serval

With its small head, spotted coat, and long legs, the African serval looks rather like a small cheetah. A good climber, it hunts small animals and catches birds. Servals always prefer to live near water.

Sand cat

The rarely seen sand cat lives in the Sahara and the deserts of western Asia. During the heat of the day, it sleeps in a dune burrow or under scrub. At night, it comes out to hunt lizards and mice. It can survive without water, getting sufficient liquid from its prey. The sand cat has thick, furry pads on its feet, so it can move fast over soft sand, and its yellow-brown coat blends into the desert.

Short, ringed tail with dark tip

Very long front legs good for speed

Short, dense fur keeps the cat warm at night and cool in the day

Black-footed cat

This fierce cat is the smallest of all wildcats. Named after the black soles of its feet, it lives in open, semi-desert country in southern Africa.

Tail is one-third of the length of the head and body

Forest felines

Most of the small cats live in woodlands, forests, or jungles and are found on every continent except Australasia. Forest cats will eat pretty much anything that they are able to catch. They are almost all very striking in appearance, with powerful, agile bodies, spotted or striped fur, and huge eyes for night hunting (pp. 16–17). They are generally silent creatures but the males try to see off their enemies by caterwauling. All the species are in danger of extinction, both from loss of habitat and also because they are still hunted for their fur, particularly in South America.

Margays
The margay looks like a smaller version of the ocelot, but it is slimmer with longer legs and tail. It feeds on birds and lives in forest trees in South America.

Leopard cat
The leopard cat is the most common wildcat in southern Asia. It looks quite like a domestic cat and is a good climber and swimmer. In China, they are known as money cats because their spots look like small coins.

Not a lotta ocelot!
Although mainly a forest cat, the ocelot is also found in grass and scrubland from Arizona to Argentina. Ocelots often live in pairs, hunt by day, and swim well. In Mexico, the ocelot is known as the "little tiger" because of its striped neck. It is the most hunted small cat in South America.

Flat-headed cat
This is a rare and elusive cat from India and parts of southeast Asia. It has dark brown fur tipped with white that gives it a silvery appearance. It appears to live along riverbanks, probably catching fish, frogs, birds, and small mammals.

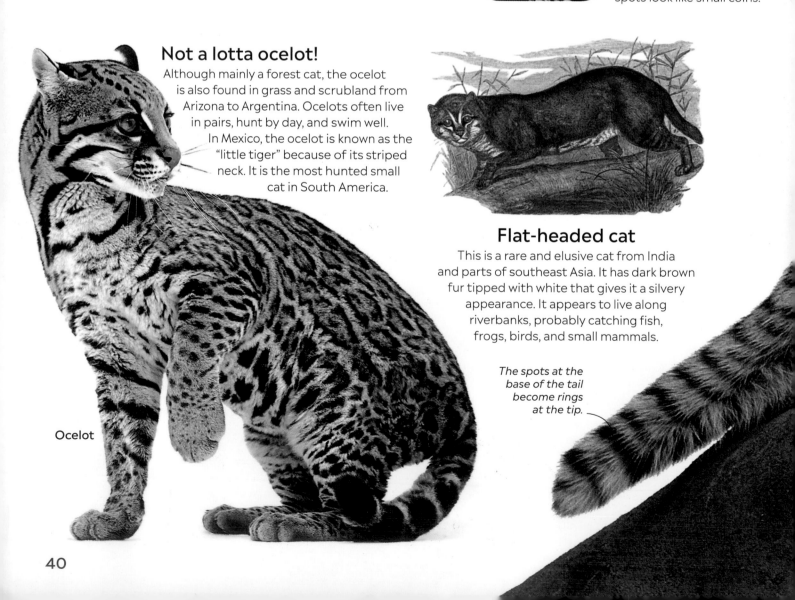

Ocelot

The spots at the base of the tail become rings at the tip.

Geoffroy's cat

Geoffroy's cat (named after its French discoverer, Etienne Geoffroy St Hilaire) lives in forests and jungles in South America. It can live at high altitudes and is known as "the mountain cat" in Argentina. It often sleeps in trees during the day.

The white ear spots are used to signal to other cats.

The dark spots are similar but smaller than those of the ocelot.

Geoffroy's cat

The claws, hidden by the soft pads, are sharpened by climbing.

Cutting back

If the destruction of the forests and jungles continues at the present rate, the balance of nature will be overturned forever and the beautiful cats that live in the forests will become extinct.

Speed king

The cheetah is the fastest land animal in the world. Unlike other cats, which are all leaping cats (pp. 10–11), the cheetah is called a running cat because it hunts fast-running animals. So it is in a different group from all other cats and has a different Latin name, *Acinonyx jubatus*. The cheetah stalks its prey in the usual way, but then, at very high speed, it will chase after the gazelle or antelope and kill it with a sharp bite to the neck. It also preys on hares, guinea fowl, and even ostriches. The female cheetah lives alone, allowing males near only when she comes on heat (p. 24). Male cheetahs often live in small groups, but only the dominant male will mate with a female.

Merger
The king cheetah of southern Africa is a very rare variety. The spots on its coat join up to form stripes on its back.

No cover up
The cheetah needs to have extended claws when running to help it grip the ground. So, unlike other cats, the cheetah does not have a protective sheath over each claw. They also do not have retractable claws.

All furred up
Cheetahs have thicker fur on the neck and shoulders. It forms a sort of "mane" that can be seen in cubs, but not in adults.

Silvery-grey fur on the back helps camouflage

Guarding cheetahs
US zoologist Laurie Marker (far right) founded the Cheetah Conservation Fund in Namibia in 1990 as she wanted to build a research centre for cheetahs. She has worked extensively on conserving the species and reintroduced captive cheetahs into the wild. She has even persuaded Namibian livestock farmers to stop killing cheetahs.

Rare animal

Cheetahs are becoming very rare. In wildlife parks, they are disturbed by tourists, and they are still being killed by poachers for their fur. Cheetahs used to be found across Africa and into India, but today they live mainly in Namibia and Zimbabwe.

Supple, muscular back

Powerful hindquarters

Striped tail is more than half the length of the head and body

No contest

The acceleration of a cheetah is comparable to this powerful Ferrari, although the animal can only keep up its speed for about 170 m (558 ft).

Narrow, dog-like paws

Fast forward

The cheetah's long legs and flexible backbone enable it to run at speeds of up to 96 kph (60 mph). From a standing start, it can reach its top speed in three seconds. Cheetah hunt by day and usually drag the carcasses into bushes to hide them from other animals.

Slender, long legs

Wandering ways

The female hides her cubs in long grass while they are very young. She does not have a permanent den but moves the cubs around every few days.

Female cheetahs look after cubs for 16–24 months

Cats' **kin**

The many different breeds of domestic cat are descended from one wild species called *Felis lybica*, the African wildcat. This small cat can be found in the African savanna and parts of Asia. In northern Europe, the European wildcat *Felis silvestris* has a stocky body and thick fur to cope with the cold climates. In Africa, the cat has a finer body, longer legs, and short hair. In India, the Indian desert cat *Felis silvestris ornata* lives in hot, dry country, and is usually spotted. The wildcat shows many slight colour variations, and the female is usually paler than the male.

Broader head and longer face than a domestic cat's

Wild in the highlands

The European wildcat can be found in small numbers in Scottish forests, but it is in danger of extinction here because it interbreeds with domestic cats that are living wild (pp. 60–61).

Scottish wildcat

Shortish tail with blunt end

Wee wildcats

Kittens go hunting with their mother at about 12 weeks and are independent at about five months. Scottish wildcat kittens have proved very difficult to tame.

Out of Africa

African wildcats live in a range of habitats across Africa. They are not as shy as other wildcats and often live close to villages, interbreeding with domestic cats.

Asian wildcat

The Indian desert cat interbreeds with the northern wildcat, the African wildcat, and the domestic cat. It has a long, black-tipped tail and the soles of its feet are black. It lives in hot, dry places and hunts mice and lizards.

Ragged ears probably indicate many battles

Domestic cat

The domestic tabby is not very different from its wild ancestor in its looks and behaviour.

Close relatives

The civet and the genet are not true cats, although they behave like them. They are carnivores and belong to the mongoose family. Their heads look similar to those of cats, but their skulls are different.

Genet
Although its head is similar to a cat's, the genet's tail is very different.

Civet
The civet and the genet live in forests and hunt at night. They have spotted or striped bodies.

Indian desert cat

The taming of the cat

Mummified cat wrapped in linen

Mummified moggy

When one of the sacred cats of Ancient Egypt died, its body was mummified (treated to prevent decay), wrapped in bandages, and placed in a special tomb.

Cats probably began living near human settlements to catch the rats and mice that were feeding on stored grain. People soon saw that cats were useful and encouraged them to remain. Recent studies show that cats first started living with humans around 10,000 years ago. Archaeologists have discovered the remains of a cat buried next to a human in a 9,500-year-old grave in Cyprus. It could be one of the world's first domesticated cats. At the height of the Egyptian civilization 3,000 years ago, the cat was already a common domestic animal and eventually it became one of the most sacred animals in Egypt. Today, domestic cats live with humans nearly everywhere in the world.

Persian puss

The fluffy, longhaired cat from Persia (now Iran) belongs to one of the oldest breeds of domestic cat, although this pot from the 13th century looks like a spotted cat rather the longhaired breed (pp. 56–57). Most longhaired pedigree cats today are descended from cats brought from Turkey and Iran in the 18th and 19th centuries.

Cat figurine decorated with calligraphic markings

Egyptian mau

Ancient image

The spotted Egyptian mau is a domestic cat from Egypt. "Mau" is the Ancient Egyptian word for cat. This is a new breed that first came to Europe in the 1950s, although with its graceful body, green eyes, and pale coat, it looks very similar to the cats of Ancient Egypt.

Perfectly preserved

This mosaic of a cat with a bird was buried by volcanic ash when Mount Vesuvius erupted in Italy in 79 CE. It was found in almost perfect condition.

46

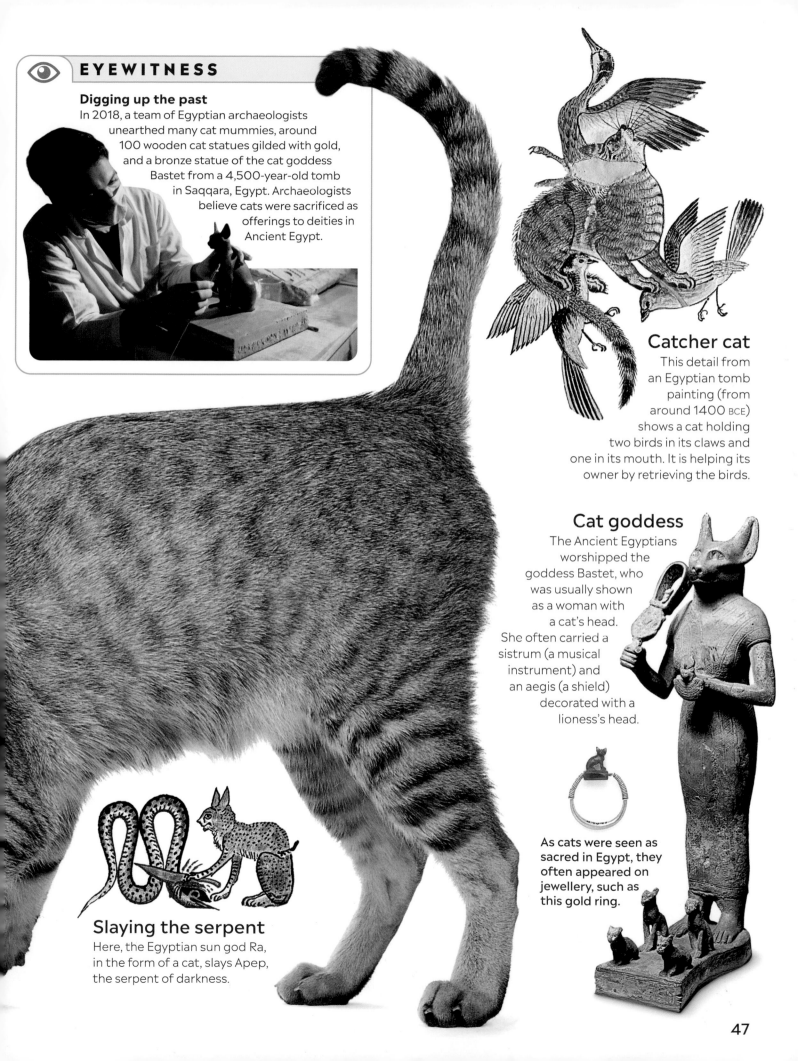

Digging up the past
In 2018, a team of Egyptian archaeologists unearthed many cat mummies, around 100 wooden cat statues gilded with gold, and a bronze statue of the cat goddess Bastet from a 4,500-year-old tomb in Saqqara, Egypt. Archaeologists believe cats were sacrificed as offerings to deities in Ancient Egypt.

Catcher cat
This detail from an Egyptian tomb painting (from around 1400 BCE) shows a cat holding two birds in its claws and one in its mouth. It is helping its owner by retrieving the birds.

Cat goddess
The Ancient Egyptians worshipped the goddess Bastet, who was usually shown as a woman with a cat's head. She often carried a sistrum (a musical instrument) and an aegis (a shield) decorated with a lioness's head.

As cats were seen as sacred in Egypt, they often appeared on jewellery, such as this gold ring.

Slaying the serpent
Here, the Egyptian sun god Ra, in the form of a cat, slays Apep, the serpent of darkness.

Myths and legends

Cats have always played a major role in folklore. This may be because they are such mysterious creatures: in the daytime they are often sleepy and affectionate, but at night they turn into stealthy, silent hunters. Many cats were killed in Europe in the late Middle Ages because they were thought to be linked with witchcraft. But in eastern countries, such as Myanmar (Burma), their magical powers were praised. Cats were welcomed at sea too, because many sailors believed that they could forecast storms.

Haunting tale

In Japan, people believe that cats have the power to turn into spirits when they die. This may be because in the Buddhist religion, the body of the cat is the temporary resting place of the soul of very spiritual people.

Blessed Birman

The Birman is the sacred cat of Myanmar. According to legend, the transformation of a white temple cat into a Birman helped to save a sacred temple from attack.

Cat chariot

During the early Renaissance period in Europe, cats were widely persecuted by the Christian Church. This was perhaps because of interest in the pagan Norse love goddess Freya, whose chariot was drawn by cats.

Familiar cats

In medieval times, the cat was thought to be a witch's "familiar" (her private connection with the devil). Many people also thought that witches could turn themselves into cats. Thousands of cats were burned in parts of Europe during this period.

Bond cat

Ernst Blofeld, the archenemy of spy James Bond, always had a white Persian cat at his side.

British black shorthair

Black magic

Belief as to whether a black cat brings good or bad luck varies. In Britain, a black cat crossing your path brings good luck, while in some American states, it is good luck if a black cat visits your house, but bad luck if it stays.

Puss-in-Boots

In southern France, there was once a belief in matagots or magician cats. One of the most famous was Puss-in-Boots, created by Charles Perrault.

Aristocats

In the mid-19th century, it became fashionable to own exotic cats, and clubs were formed to set standards and compare breeds. During the 20th century, many breeds were developed that look very different from the cat's wild ancestor. But whatever the breed, the basic behavioural patterns of cats remain the same. For a cat to be affectionate, it must be handled and talked to from birth. If kittens are reared in a cattery in large numbers, and then taken from their mother at six weeks old to be placed with a family, they may appear neurotic. This is due to a lack of human contact and because they have been taken from their mother too soon.

EYEWITNESS

First show
In 1871, Harrison Weir (1824–1906) staged the first modern cat show in London, UK. A Persian kitten won. He founded the National Cat Club in 1887 and served as its president and show manager until 1890. His illustrated book *Our Cats and All About Them* (1889) describes the pedigree cat breeds of his time.

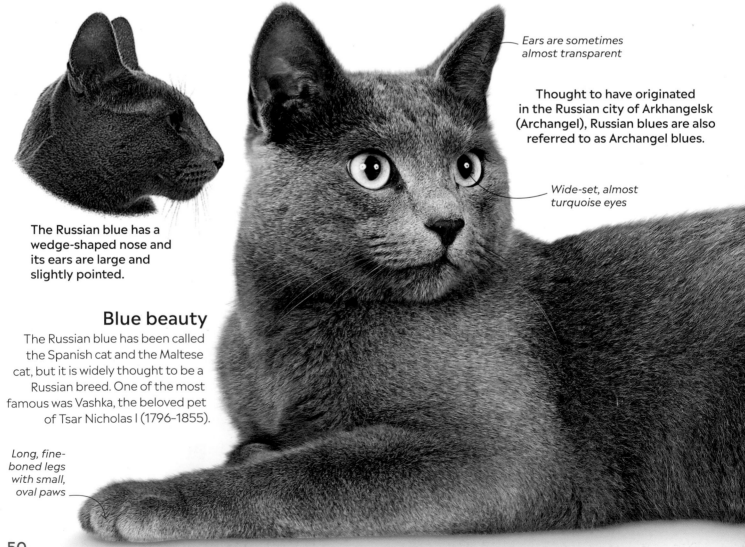

Ears are sometimes almost transparent

Thought to have originated in the Russian city of Arkhangelsk (Archangel), Russian blues are also referred to as Archangel blues.

Wide-set, almost turquoise eyes

The Russian blue has a wedge-shaped nose and its ears are large and slightly pointed.

Blue beauty
The Russian blue has been called the Spanish cat and the Maltese cat, but it is widely thought to be a Russian breed. One of the most famous was Vashka, the beloved pet of Tsar Nicholas I (1796–1855).

Long, fine-boned legs with small, oval paws

Large, round, copper-coloured eyes

Thickset body

Deep orange coat

Small, rounded ears

Red self longhair

Short, solid legs

Fit and fluffed-up
Grooming longhaired cats is very important, particularly before a cat show. It prevents tangling and gets rid of excess hair (p. 62).

Unlucky 13
In 1898, a party of 13 dined at London's Savoy Hotel. The first guest to leave was killed soon after, fulfilling an old superstition. At the Savoy today, Kaspar, the wooden cat, always sits at the table when there are 13 diners.

Red self longhair
Red self longhairs are a fairly rare breed. The beautiful red coat should show no shading or tabby markings.

The nose of the red self is so flat that the cat sometimes has trouble breathing through it.

Show cats are judged based on breed standards.

Rosettes

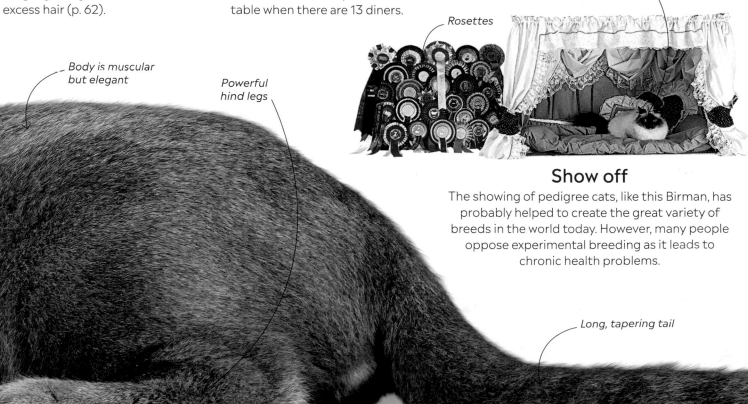

Show off
The showing of pedigree cats, like this Birman, has probably helped to create the great variety of breeds in the world today. However, many people oppose experimental breeding as it leads to chronic health problems.

Body is muscular but elegant

Powerful hind legs

Long, tapering tail

Shorthairs

To this day, most cats have short hair (longhairs appeared only 500 years ago). This was because a cat could survive and fend for itself more easily if its coat was short. Pedigree shorthaired cats fall into three main groups: the British, American, and the Oriental shorthair. The British shorthair is a stocky, muscular cat with shortish legs. The American shorthair is larger and more lithe and has slightly longer legs. Among the most popular cats today are the sleek Oriental shorthairs, which include the Siamese, Burmese, and Abyssinian breeds. There are also many non-pedigree shorthaired cats of all shapes and sizes.

American portraits, like this one by Ammi Phillips (1788–1865), often included the family pet.

Sew much fun

In the early 20th century, kittens were often used to illustrate birthday cards and postcards. Kittens still enjoy playing with cotton reels today.

Abyssinian

The graceful Abyssinian is believed to have originated in Abyssinia (present-day Ethiopia). It comes in many colours including brown, sorrel (light copper), blue, fawn, lilac (pinkish-grey), and silver.

Large, pointed ears set far apart

Almond-shaped green eyes

Small, oval-shaped paws with black pads

Longish tail tipped with black

Large ears set high on the head

Continued on next page

Tortoiseshell and white coat covers thickset body

Heart-shaped face with very round, bright green eyes

Rare coat

Tortoiseshell and white cats are almost always female and very hard to breed. To produce a tortoiseshell, females are best mated to a solid-coloured black, red, or cream male, but even then there may be only one, or no kittens with the desired colouring. A male cat born with these colours is usually unable to breed.

Fur separates when the back is bent

Look-out

This tabby has found a good perch. Non-pedigree cats are often less nervous than highly bred cats and usually make good pets.

Small, oval paws with blue to lavender-coloured pads

Korat

The dusky-blue korat is one of the oldest breeds of cat and originally comes from Thailand. The breed was first taken to the USA in the 1950s, but did not arrive in Britain until the 1970s. It is a gentle, rather nervous cat.

Burmese

Like the Abyssinian, the Burmese has a variety of coat colours. Brown Burmese were living in temples in Myanmar as long ago as the 15th century. It is an affectionate, intelligent cat that loves to lie on beds.

Mr and Mrs Clark and Percy

There is no doubt that artists like painting cats. This famous painting from 1970–1971 by British artist David Hockney shows his friends Ossie Clark and Celia Birtwell with their large, white cat Percy taking a central role.

Two's company

Tabby coats are the most common markings in non-pedigree cats. Highly bred cats are often less robust than non-pedigree cats, because inbreeding (p. 13) can cause physical weaknesses. These two cats clearly get on well. They are showing no aggressive signs to each other.

Ginger and white cat

Ringed, fluffy tail

Mr Mistoffelees

Old Possum's Book of Practical Cats (1939) by T S Eliot describes many wonderful cats. Mr Mistoffelees (like all black cats pp. 48–49) has his own share of magic.

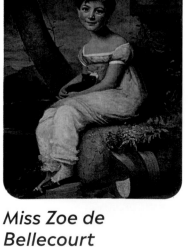

Miss Zoe de Bellecourt

This portrait was painted by Scottish artist George Watson (1767–1837). Cats were seen as suitable pets for young ladies.

Colour change

People have tried to produce all-black and all-white versions of the Russian blue. The breed is most popular in New Zealand.

Thin, tapering tail

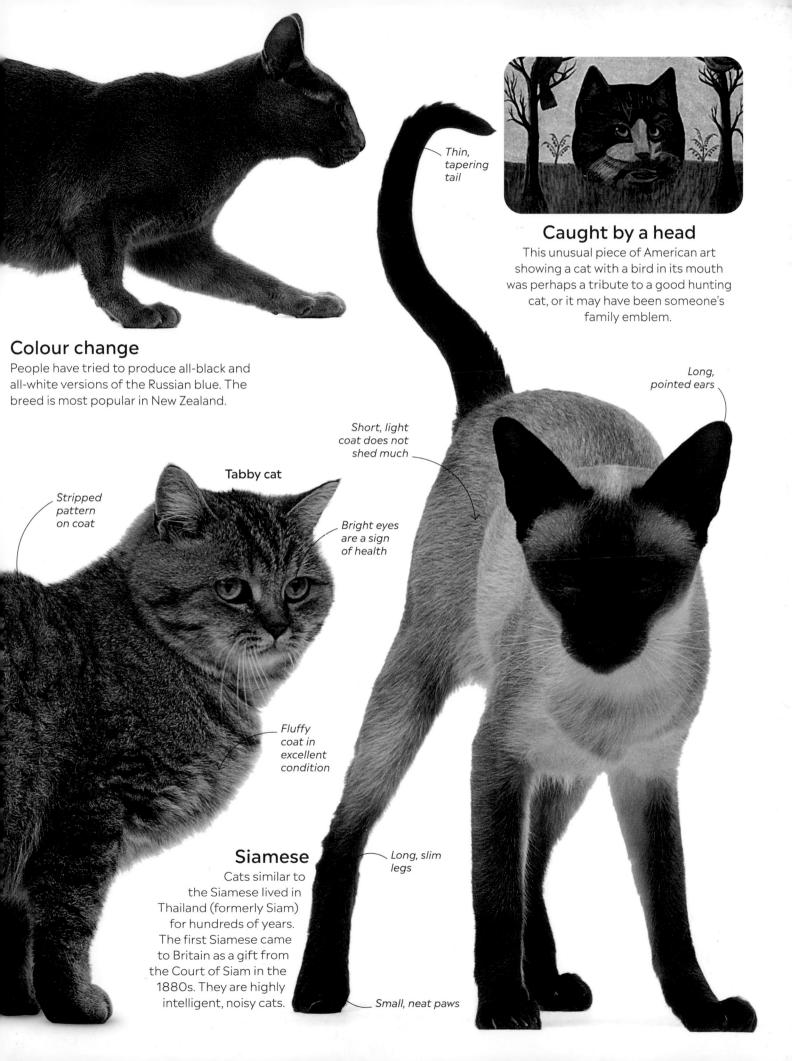

Caught by a head

This unusual piece of American art showing a cat with a bird in its mouth was perhaps a tribute to a good hunting cat, or it may have been someone's family emblem.

Long, pointed ears

Short, light coat does not shed much

Bright eyes are a sign of health

Stripped pattern on coat

Tabby cat

Fluffy coat in excellent condition

Siamese

Cats similar to the Siamese lived in Thailand (formerly Siam) for hundreds of years. The first Siamese came to Britain as a gift from the Court of Siam in the 1880s. They are highly intelligent, noisy cats.

Long, slim legs

Small, neat paws

Longhairs

All wildcats have a two-layer fur coat (p. 14),
and in cold countries, cats tend to have thicker,
longer fur. Long hair would be a disadvantage
to a wildcat because it would become matted
and tangled in bushes. Among the oldest
breeds of longhaired cats are the Persian and
the Angora (originally from Turkey). Longhaired cats are usually
placid and make excellent companions, but they do need more
grooming than shorthaired cats.

Famous French artist, author, and cat lover Jean Cocteau (1889–1963) designed this logo.

Colour woodcut by American artist Elizabeth Norton (1887–1985)

Angora

This is an early engraving of an Angora, possibly the first longhair to be seen in Europe.

Small, round head with wide-set ears

Neck ruff

Long, feathery tail

Short head with long, pink-tipped nose

Turkish Vans

This cat is often called the Turkish swimming cat because it is fond of playing in water. It is named after the area around Lake Van in Turkey, where it has been bred for several hundred years.

Frowning expression caused by horizontal crease between the eyes

Birman

The Birman has a longer body than a typical longhair, and similar markings to a Siamese. It may, in fact, be a cross between a Siamese and a Persian. These cats always have white feet.

Red self

Although this breed was shown in Britain at the end of the 19th century (pp. 50–51), all pedigree cat breeding dwindled during World Wars I and II, and the red self has become rare in Europe.

Blunt-ended, plume-like tail

Maine coon

The Maine coon is the oldest American breed of cat. According to tradition, it used to roam free in the state of Maine and was often compared with the raccoon, which has similar markings. In fact, it most likely descends from American farm cats and longhaired cats brought by boat from Europe.

Maine coon can reach 102 cm (40 in) in length

Pallas's cat

This wildcat was discovered by German naturalist Peter Simon Pallas (1741–1811) in the area around the Caspian Sea, in the Soviet Union. It has a very thick, long coat, which helps to protect it from the harsh climate of its habitat.

Strong legs, with large, round paws

Short and stout legs

Curious cats

The breeding of cats for special characteristics (selective breeding) began at the start of the 20th century (pp. 50–51). Since then, many different breeds have been developed. Almost any part of the cat can be altered by selective breeding. For example, cats can be bred with very fluffy fur or a short tail. Sometimes curiosities in the wild, like the white tiger, are perfectly healthy, as are some new domestic breeds like the Burmilla, a cross between a Burmese and a Chinchilla Persian. But, all too often, excessive inbreeding produces animals with serious health issues.

Cheshire cat

The British writer Lewis Carroll (1832–1898) immortalized the grinning Cheshire Cat in his book *Alice's Adventures in Wonderland*.

The Sphynx

Hairless kittens are sometimes born due to a genetic abnormality. One such kitten, born in 1966 to a black and white cat, was used to develop a new breed of hairless cat called the Sphynx.

Striking eyes

In some cats, the two eyes are in different colours – a natural condition known as heterochromia. Usually, one iris is blue and the other is green, yellow, or brown.

The white coat occurs in as few as one in 10,000 wild tigers.

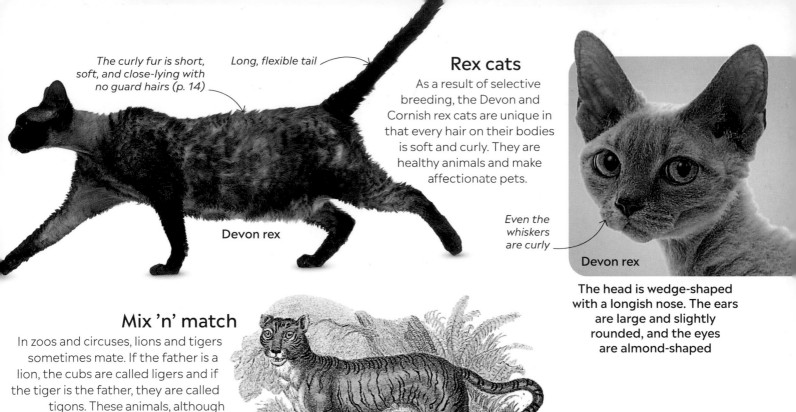

The curly fur is short, soft, and close-lying with no guard hairs (p. 14)

Long, flexible tail

Devon rex

Rex cats

As a result of selective breeding, the Devon and Cornish rex cats are unique in that every hair on their bodies is soft and curly. They are healthy animals and make affectionate pets.

Even the whiskers are curly

Devon rex

The head is wedge-shaped with a longish nose. The ears are large and slightly rounded, and the eyes are almond-shaped

Mix 'n' match

In zoos and circuses, lions and tigers sometimes mate. If the father is a lion, the cubs are called ligers and if the tiger is the father, they are called tigons. These animals, although healthy, are often infertile (unable to produce cubs). However, one liger did mate successfully in Germany.

Manx cats can have no tail at all, a tiny bump, a moveable tail stump, or a small tail.

White tiger

The striking white tiger was once not uncommon in north and east central India, although there are few there now. The unusual colour is a natural occurrence.

Well-defined patches of black, cream, orange, and white fur

White tigers have blue eyes instead of green or yellow like normal tigers

Manx

Kittens without tails can be born in any litter. Tailless cats called Manx became common on the Isle of Man off the English coast more than 200 years ago, probably as a result of the island's geographical isolation, and inbreeding (p. 13).

Strong back legs

Street life

All cities have a secret world of teeming animal life. City cats find plenty of pigeons, rats, mice, and cockroaches in alleys, dustbins, and drains. City-dwelling cats have their own territories, crawling into basements, under sheds, or up onto roofs. Male city (alley) cats mark and defend their territory in the same way as pet cats and wildcats. Females also have territories, and find hidden places to have their kittens. Cats are useful in cities because they get rid of rubbish and pests. However, the population of city cats can become too large if too many people feed them, and this upsets the balance of the concrete jungle.

Trap-Neuter-Return

Many communities run trap-neuter-return (TNR) programmes. People take stray cats to veterinarians to be neutered under proper medical care so that they cannot breed any more. This keeps feral population under control. The ear tips of these cats are usually taken off to help identify them as neutered.

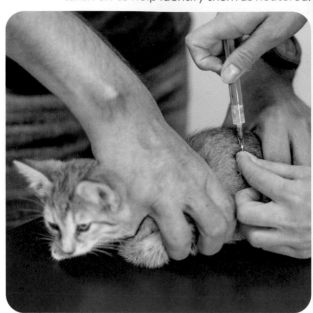

 EYEWITNESS

Kitten love

Known as the Kitten Lady, Hannah Shaw rescues stray kittens in the USA, especially orphaned ones. Once they are healthy, she finds homes for them. She has written books about caring for kittens and raises awareness globally through social media.

Illustration from *Public and Private Life of Animals*

Cats on a hot tin roof

Their roaming natures often mean that cats take to the rooftops. Here, they can escape from humans and gain access to interesting places. This delightful scene is by French artist Grandville (1803–1847).

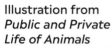

Ragged tail

Street cats

It is not easy to tell the difference between pet cats that go out at night, and street cats that have little or no human contact. Street cats are usually rather nervous and scruffy. They run away when approached, and may be grubby, with torn ears and sore places from frequent battles.

Ear is ragged and scarred, a certain sign of battles fought

Coat is slightly matted, a sign that this cat is not in peak condition

No two the same

When a female cat is on heat (p. 24), several males may mate with her. This can mean that there is more than one father of the kittens in a litter, and they can all look very different, as in the painting above.

Feral cats

Feral refers to domestic animals that no longer live with humans and have returned to the wild. Some alley cats living in cities have become feral. Feral cats are often found on sparsely populated islands where they were left by sailors.

Alley cat
There is a fine line between an alley cat and a feral cat. Some alley cats can live without human control, but most depend on humans in some way.

Caring for cats

Cats are true individuals with their own needs. If possible, every cat should be allowed outside to explore its territory and also to eat the blades of grass that help its digestion. Magnetic cat flaps allow cats maximum freedom, as the flap is opened by a magnet on the collar. Most people get their cats neutered, which prevents them from producing litters of unwanted kittens. Cats also need to be vaccinated against harmful diseases such as cat flu. Cats can live for over 20 years and need constant care. They make very rewarding pets.

Kittens and puppies often appeared on Victorian cards.

Kat kit
Regular brushing prevents cats, especially longhairs, from swallowing hair when they lick themselves. Hair forms a fur-ball in the stomach, which can make a cat ill.

Water bowl

Stretch mat
Every cat needs to stretch its body (p. 27). Mats or scratching posts are ideal for this.

Moggy menu
Cats are carnivores and need to eat meat or fish daily. Hard cat biscuits help to keep the teeth and jaws healthy. Water is also essential.

Food bowl

Scoop

Gravel or commercial cat litter

Litter tray

Creature comforts
Cats are territorial and need their own sleeping place. They often choose beds or chairs because they smell reassuring.

Digging in
Nearly all cats can be trained to use a litter tray. The cat buries its waste, but the litter needs to be cleaned out and changed daily,

Playtime
Cats love to play and exercise. Toys should not contain any loose string that could wind round the cat or strangle it.

Collared
Quick-release buckle collars can be removed easily if the collar gets caught in a branch or twig. In large towns, it is advisable to have one with an identification disc attached.

Front grill can be securely fastened

On the road
Cats hate to be taken away from their own territory. Many owners leave cats in their own home with someone coming in to feed them when they go on holiday. If this is not possible, a secure travelling basket, with a favourite blanket in it, is important.

Basket case
Cats like to sleep in places that smell of their owner. So the cat basket should be lined with newspaper to prevent draughts, and then covered with an old item of clothing as a "security blanket". Keep sleeping places free from fleas by regular spraying or washing with a special insecticide.

All you need is love
Cats need affection, and they display love for their owners in return. Cat ownership has been shown to benefit humans, particularly the old and lonely. Each cat wants different levels of interaction. Their refusal to socialize must be respected.

Did you **know?**

AMAZING FACTS

Ridged nose pad

The cat's nose pad has a unique pattern, just like a human fingerprint.

There are more than 500 million domestic cats in the world.

A cat's heart beats nearly twice as fast as a human heart.

Cats are partially colour blind. They can mainly see blues and yellows with smaller amounts of red and green.

In just seven years, a single pair of cats and their offspring could produce 420,000 kittens.

Sir Isaac Newton, who discovered the laws of gravity, also invented the cat flap.

The flat-headed cat is an expert fisher. Its webbed paws and well-developed premolars grip slippery prey well.

The domestic cat is the only cat to hold its tail vertically while walking. Wildcats hold their tails horizontally or between their legs.

A cat holding its tail tall

Cats can see brilliantly at dawn and dusk, which are excellent hunting times. They can see well in dim light because a layer of cells called the "tapetum lucidum" at the back of their eyes reflects light back through the retina.

A cat's ear can turn up to 180 degrees. Each ear has more than 20 muscles to control this movement.

Almost all tortoiseshell cats are female because the colouring is linked to the female sex gene.

On average, cats spend two-thirds of every day sleeping. So a nine-year-old cat has been awake for only three years of its life.

Cats "meow" often at humans, but hardly ever "meow" at other cats.

A cat nap

The spots on the back of the African cheetah are so large that they join to form striking black stripes running down its spine.

A cat cannot see things that are immediately under its nose, as its nose gets in the way.

A person who killed a cat in Ancient Egypt could be put to death.

The clouded leopard's canine teeth can be as long as 4.5 cm (1.8 in).

The average cat-food meal is equivalent to about five mice.

Cats spend nearly one-third of their waking hours grooming themselves.

According to Hebrew folklore, Noah was afraid that rats would eat all the food he had stored in the ark, so God made the lion sneeze, and out popped a cat.

A cat hard at work grooming itself

A cat's colourpoint pattern – where the ears, face, legs, and tail are darker than the main body – is affected by temperature. The pattern is caused by a gene that prevents colour in warm parts of the body and allows colour in cooler areas, such as the face, ears, and tail.

The world's oldest domestic cat to be recorded was Creme Puff, who lived for 38 years.

The clouded leopard

QUESTIONS AND ANSWERS

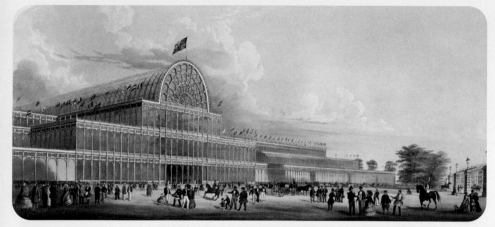

Crystal Palace, London

Where was the first formal cat show?

It was held at Crystal Palace in London, UK, on 13 July 1871.

Why does a cat wag its tail?

A cat will swish its tail when annoyed, move it rapidly when agitated, and twitch it when excited.

How well can a cat smell?

A cat can smell another cat 100 m (330 ft) away. Cats smell with their nose, but also use the Jacobson's organ, in the roof of the mouth.

How many claws does a cat have?

Cats have five clawed toes on the front paws and four on the back.

What colours are cats' eyes?

Cats' eyes can be copper, orange, lavender, blue, or yellow. Some cats are odd-eyed, so each eye has a different colour.

How long do cats usually live?

Domestic cats can live up to 20 years with good veterinary care.

Why do cats rub against people's legs?

When cats rub against people, they are marking them with their scent glands, which are between their eyes and ears, and near their tail.

Cats like to rub against people

Chartreux cats have orange eyes

How many teeth do cats have?

Adult cats have a total of 30 teeth, for grasping, cutting, and shredding food. Kittens have 26 temporary teeth, which they lose when they are about six months old.

What makes it possible for cats to get through small spaces?

A cat's head is its bulkiest bony structure. If it is able to get its head through, it can squeeze the rest of its body through a small gap.

Cat squeezing through a small space

RECORD BREAKERS

Mother to the most kittens
A cat called "Dusty" holds the record for the largest number of kittens. She had more than 420 kittens in her lifetime.

The world's best "mouser"
"Towser", a tabby working on pest control in Scotland caught 28,899 mice in 21 years, an average of about four each day.

The largest cat breed
The largest cat breed is the Maine coon. Males weigh between 6.8 and 11.3 kg (15 to 25 lb), while females weigh between 3.6 and 5.4 kg (8 to 12 lb).

The smallest cat breed
The smallest cat breed is the Singapura. Males weigh about 2.7 kg (6 lb); females weigh about 1.8 kg (4 lb).

A Singapura kitten

Identifying breeds

Since selective breeding began, the look of some breeds has changed considerably. Set standards describe the ideal appearance of a breed. New cat breeds can result from crossing two established breeds, or a domestic cat with a small wildcat.

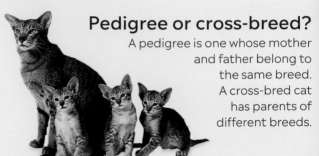

Pedigree or cross-breed?

A pedigree is one whose mother and father belong to the same breed. A cross-bred cat has parents of different breeds.

Mother and kittens

Hair length

Cats fall into one of three groups, depending on the length of their hair. Longhaired cats have a thick coat that can make them appear twice their actual size. The fur of shorthaired cats may be fine or coarse, and the hairs may be straight, crinkled, curly, or wavy. The Sphynx is the only pedigree breed that is "hairless".

The Maine coon, a longhaired cat

The British blue shorthair

The "hairless" Sphynx

Cat breeds

The Governing Council of the Cat Fancy (GCCF) recognizes the following groups of cat breeds.

Semi-longhairs
Some semi-longhairs, such as the Turkish Van, have a thinner undercoat than longhaired cats.

Cream Turkish Van

Turkish Vans are regarded as Turkey's national treasure.

British shorthairs
British shorthairs exist in a wide range of colours and patterns. They have a large, rounded body shape and round faces.

Orange-eyed white Persian longhair

Persian longhairs
Persian longhairs have long, dense fur, flat faces, and small ears.

The strongest point colour is on the tail and the head.

Cream point British shorthair

Colours and patterns

Over the years, selective breeding (pp. 58–59) has established a variety of different patterns and colours within the recognized breeds.

Tortie and white

Parti-coloured coats have two or more definite colours, such as black and white. Tortoiseshell coats are black, red, and cream.

Tortie smoke longhair

Smoke coats have a white undercoat covered by a dark colour, such as black, blue, or red.

Tabby coats have symmetrical patterns of stripes and spots of a dark colour on a lighter background.

Black

Shaded coats are like smoke coats except that the dark colour occurs only on the tips of the hairs.

Solid (or self) coats are one colour only – black, blue, brown, cream (tan), lilac (light grey), red, or white.

Red shaded cameo

Silver spotted tabby

Fawn Abyssinian

Ticked coats have bands of colour on each hair, creating a wavy effect.

Chocolate point Siamese

Pointed coats have a solid colour on the main part of the cat's body, and a darker colour on the extremities.

Foreign cats
This group includes a range of different cats. The Tiffanie has silky, fine hair. Asian cats have short, close-lying fur. The Ocicat has Siamese and Abyssinian ancestry. The Cornish rex has short, curly hair, and the Singapura has a ticked coat.

Siamese
Siamese cats also have wedge-shaped faces and large, wide ears. They have long, light-coloured bodies with darker extremities.

Cream Burmese

Red Tiffanie

Burmese cats
Burmese have short, glossy fur, muscular bodies, and thin legs. They can be solid colours or tortoiseshell.

Blue point Siamese

Find out more

Even if you do not have a cat of your own, there are many ways of finding out more about them. You could join a cat club and go along to shows to find out about different breeds. You can also find out information from your local cat charity. If you find big cats interesting, visit a wildlife park to see lions, leopards, or tigers in action.

Cat shows

Cat shows take place all year round, often on Saturdays, and are usually open to the public in the afternoon. At least 1,500 cats take part in the annual GCCF Supreme Show in November.

The judges, dressed in white, examine the cats exhibited at a show.

A cat of your own

If you are considering getting a cat, investigate first the kind of home and care a cat needs. The RSPCA and the Governing Council of the Cat Fancy (GCCF) provide information to help you make the decision.

Cats belonging to the club may have won many awards

Cute kittens

Pedigree kittens stay with their mother until they are 13 weeks old, and for at least a week after they have had their vaccinations. It is best to not separate kittens from their mothers for at least eight weeks, so that they are fully protected before they go to a new home.

The kitten feels safe near its family.

Join a cat club

The GCCF can tell you where your nearest cat club is. Clubs organize and take part in shows at which club members can exhibit their cats. There are more than 150 cat clubs in the UK.

Oriental shorthair cats have large ears and a wedge-shaped head.

PLACES TO VISIT

THE CAT ASSOCIATION OF BRITAIN CAT OF THE YEAR SHOW
• The Cat Association of Britain is the British member of FIFe, the Fédération Internationale Féline, which covers 37 countries.
• The CA organizes The Cat of the Year Show in January each year. Check the website **www.cfainc.org**

WHIPSNADE WILD ANIMAL PARK, UK
• Set in 600 acres (240 hectares) of parkland, this is one of Europe's largest conservation parks, with over 2,500 animals. For more information, see **www.zsl.org/zsl-whipsnade-zoo**

LONGLEAT SAFARI PARK, UK
• Opened in 1966, Longleat was the first drive-through safari park outside Africa. For further details, go to the website **www.longleat.co.uk**

SAN DIEGO ZOO SAFARI PARK, USA
• Located in California, this safari park offers a wide range of experiences, such as open-air safari, cart safari, and flightline safari, where people can zipline as high as 40 m (130 ft) above the ground and view the wildlife in savannah habitats. For further details, go to the website **www.sdzsafaripark.org**

Big cats

One way to learn more about big cats is to go along to wildlife parks and talk to the keepers. Find out more from the website **www.safaripark.co.uk**

The animals are used to visitors in their cars.

Stray cats

There are charities that take care of injured and stray cats and find suitable new homes for them. Cats Protection help more than 200,000 cats each year. The RSPCA also rescues and rehouses large numbers of cats.

USEFUL WEBSITES

• For information on the GCCF, see:
www.gccfcats.org
• To find details of the Cat Association of Britain, go to:
www.cfainc.org
• For a wealth of information on pedigree cats in the UK, go to:
https://www.pedigreecatworld.co.uk/breed-info/
• To find out about the PDSA, a charity that provides a free veterinary service for pets of people in need, see:
www.pdsa.org.uk
• For information on Cats Protection, go to:
www.cats.org.uk
• Find out about the work of the RSPCA at:
www.rspca.org.uk/home
• To find out more about the Wildlife Conservation Society, an organization that aims to conserve both wildlife and the world's largest wild places, see:
www.wcs.org
• For a wealth of information about big cats, see:
www.bornfree.org.uk

Glossary

BREED A group of cats with particular characteristics. Humans control breeding to achieve specific features, such as coat type or head shape.

CAMOUFLAGE The coloration of an animal that either blends in with the colour of the surroundings or breaks up the animal's outline with stripes or spots, making it harder to see.

CANINE TEETH Four large, pointed teeth, two in the upper jaw and two in the lower. They are used to stab prey.

CARNASSIAL TEETH The teeth at the side of the jaw used for cutting off meat.

The four large canine teeth

CARNIVORE A member of the order Carnivora, which contains animals that have teeth for biting and shearing flesh. Carnivores mostly eat meat.

CATERWAUL A howling, wailing cry made by a female cat when it is on heat.

CLASS A class contains one or more orders. Cats are part of the class Mammalia.

CLAW A curved, sharp, pointed nail on the toe. Cats draw in, or retract, their claws when they are relaxed, but can extend them quickly. Only the cheetah cannot retract its claws.

CROSS-BREEDING The mating of two different breeds.

DOUBLE COAT A long top-coat over a short undercoat.

DOWN HAIR The soft, fine hair that makes up a short undercoat and provides body insulation.

FAMILY Any of the taxonomic groups into which an order is divided. A family contains one or more genera. Felidae is the name of the cat family.

FELINE Cat or catlike.

FERAL CATS Domestic cats that have returned to living in the wild and live totally outside human control.

FORELEGS The front legs of a four-legged animal.

GROOM To keep clean and tidy. People groom cats, but cats also spend considerable time grooming themselves with their tongues and paws.

GUARD HAIRS Long hairs that form part of the top-coat.

HABITAT The natural home of an animal or plant.

HIND LEGS The back legs of a four-legged animal.

INBREEDING Repeated breeding within a group of animals that are closely related to each other.

JACOBSON'S ORGAN A taste-smell organ in the roof of a cat's mouth.

KITTEN A young cat. The young of some large cats are known as cubs.

LIGAMENT The tough tissue that connects bones and cartilage.

Grooming a cat at a show

LITTER A group of young born at one time to one female cat.

LONGHAIR A cat with a thick, long, double coat.

MANE Long hair growing on or around the neck.

NEUTER A cat that has had its reproductive organs surgically removed.

NOSE LEATHER The area of coloured skin, not covered by fur, on a cat's nose.

ORDER Any of the taxonomic groups into which a class is divided. An order contains one or more families. Cats belong to the order Carnivora.

PADS The leathery areas on the feet.

PAPILLAE The hard, shiny points on a cat's tongue used for grooming.

PARTI-COLOURED A cat with a coat of two or more well-defined colours.

PAW A cat's foot, with its leathery pads and sharp claws.

PEDIGREE The record of a pure-breed's ancestors.

POINTS Darker coloured areas at the body's extremities – on the legs, paws, tail, head, and ears.

A European wildcat

PURE-BREED A cat with parents belonging to the same breed. A pure-breed is also known as a pedigree cat.

PURR To make a low, vibrant sound, usually expressing pleasure. The sound is made when the bones at the base of the tongue vibrate.

SELF (or **SOLID**) A cat with a coat of only one colour.

SEMI-LONGHAIR A cat with a relatively long top-coat, but a fairly thin undercoat.

SHEATHE To allow a claw to move back inside its bony, protective structure.

SHORTHAIR A cat with a short coat.

SKELETON The framework of bones that gives shape to an animal, allows the muscles to move, protects the organs, is a source of blood cells, and provides a mineral store.

SMOKE A cat with a white undercoat and a darker top-coat.

SPECIES Any of the taxonomic groups into which a genus is divided. Members of the same species are able to breed with each other.

SPHYNX A breed of cat that is hairless apart from a little short, downy fur usually on its extremities.

SPRAYING Using urine to mark a territory. In particular, male cats that have not been neutered do this.

A cat's tongue is covered in papillae.

STALKING To approach prey stealthily.

SUCKLE To suck milk from the mother. The term also means to give milk to a young animal.

TABBY A coat with striped, blotched, spotted, or ticked markings.

TAPETUM LUCIDUM The cells at the back of a cat's eye that reflect light.

TAXONOMY Relating to the classification of organisms into groups, based on their similarities or origin.

A Turkish Van pedigree cat

TORTOISESHELL A cat (usually female) with black and red fur – white may or may not be present. In cats where white is present, they are usually detailed as tortoiseshell and white.

UNDERCOAT A coat of dense, soft fur beneath the outer, coarser fur.

VAN A coat with a white body but a coloured head and tail.

WEAN When a kitten changes from a milk diet to a meat diet.

WHISKERS The stiff hairs on a cat's face, with highly sensitive nerves at their roots.

A mother cat suckles her kittens.

TENDON A band of tough tissue that attaches a muscle to a bone.

TICKED A coat in which there are bands of different colour on each hair.

TOP-COAT The outer coat, made up of guard and awn hairs (hairs that provide insulation).

Index

Acknowledgments

The publisher would like to thank the following people for their help with making the book:
Trevor Smith and all the staff at Trevor Smith's Animal World; Jim Clubb of Clubb-Chipperfield; Nicki Barrass of Al Animals; Terry Moore of the Cat Survival Trust; the staff of the British Museum and the Natural History Museum for their assistance; Jacquie Gulliver and Lynne Williams for their work on the initial stages of the book; Christian Sévigny and Liz Sephton for design assistance; Claire Gillard and Céline Carez for editorial assistance; Hazel Beynon for text editing; Saloni Singh and Priyanka Sharma-Saddi for the jacket; and Joanna Penning for proofreading and the index.

The publisher would like to thank the following for their kind permission to reproduce their images:

(Key: a-above; b-below; c-centre; f-far; l-left; r-right; t=top; m=middle)

Alamy Stock Photo: Holger Hollemann / dpa 8br; The History Collection 10clb; All Canada Photos 14tr; Paul Biggins 16cr; Mark Burdette 21cr; Bebedi 22br; Imagebroker 23tr; Nature Picture Library 23cl; FLPA 27cr; Minden Pictures 37br; Fiona Ayerst 42bc; Robert Bradley 42bl; Martin Chapman 42–43c; Minden Pictures 43tc; Stu Porter 43tr; DPA picture alliance 47tl; Daria Kulkova 51ca; Hemis 57bc; Pictorial Press Ltd 58tl; Simon Kadula 60cra; Alex Edelman / CNP / MediaPunch 60bl; Charlie Bryan 68crb; Adrian Sherratt 69clb; **Animals Unlimited:** 53b; **Ardea:** R.Beames 40c; K. Fink 40tr; **Bridgeman Art Library:** 62tl; Bibliothèque Nationale,
Paris 28tl; Chadwick Gallery, Warwicks 52c; National Gallery, London 30tl detail; National Gallery of Scotland 54bl; Victoria & Albert Museum, London 20tr; **Courtesy of the Trustees of the British Museum:** 6tr, 22clb, 31tr; **Dreamstime.com:** Isselee 1c; Anankkml 4tl, 10–11t; Jean-marc Strydom 16tr; Andreykuzmin 21tl; Megamnogo 24bl; David Pillow 24cl; Slowmotiongli 25cr; Blair Costelloe 28–29b; Victor Lapaev 32–33tl; Abeselom Zerit 33cr; Holly Kuchera 36–37b; Claire Fulton 39bc; Ecophoto 45tl; Isselee 56–57b; Sergey Taran 58br; Vinodkumar Amberkhane 61crb; WildStrawberry_magic 63ca; Clara Shalyapina 68cl; **Getty Images:** David A. Northcott 12tl; PHILIPP ROHNER / 500px 19cb; Erich Schmidt 26bl; Express Newspapers 29tr; Pallava Bagla 31tc; Carlos Tischler / NurPhoto 35br; DE AGOSTINI PICTURE LIBRARY 38clb; Erich Schmidt 50–51b; **Getty Images/iStock:** BrettDurrant 28cl; **In the Collection of the Duke of Buccleuch & Queensberry KT:** 16cl detail; **Jean Loup Charmet:** 7tr; Jen & Des Bartlett 13c, 23bl; Jane Burton 16cb; Eric Creighton 26cl; Gerald Cubitt 43br; Hans Reinhard 12c, 16tl, 37tl; Norman Tomalin 45bl; Gunter Ziesler 42tr; **E.T. Archive:** 24tr, 62br; **Mary Evans Picture Library:** 19t, 27cr, 49tl, tr; **Werner Forman Archive:** 32cl; **Robert Harding Picture Library:** 49bl; "Mr & Mrs Clark & Percy" 1970–1, **© David Hockney/photo Tate Gallery:** 54tl; **Michael Holford:** 30clb, 31br, 34cl, 37c, 47tl, 47br, 48cl; **Hulton-Deutsch Collection:** 24tr; **Hutchison Library:** 35tr; **Images Colour Library:** 47bl; **Kobal Collection:** 22cl, 49cr; **LYNX:** 36cl; **Metropolitan Museum of Art:** 56tr; **Museum of American Folk Art:** 52tr; **National Gallery of Art, Washington:** 55tr (gift of Edgar William & Bernice Chrysler Garbisch); **naturepl.**

com: Daniel Heuclin 34–35c; **Natural History Museum:** 8tl, cb, 12bl, 13tl, br, 33cl, 34cr, 36bl; **Natural History Photographic Agency:** Agence Nature 18bl; Peter Johnson 14cl, 45cl; Gérard Lacz 58cl; **Northampton Historical Society, Mass.:** 15tc; **Oxford Scientific Films:** 37tc, 39tl; Sean Morris 41b; Richard Packwood 12cb; Kjell Sandved 59clb; Bernard Schellhammer 53cr; **Quadrant Picture Library:** 43cr; **Courtesy of The Savoy:** 51ca; **Scala:** Palazzo Medici Riccardi, Florence 32tr detail; Museo Nationale, Napoli 46tl; Survival Anglia; Dieter & Mary Plage 32tl; Alan Root 27tr; **Amoret Tanner:** 29tl; **Zefa:** 16ct; E. & P. Bauer 23bl, 38bl; M. N. Boulton 11bl; Bramaz 63br; Lummerc 20br; **Ardea London Ltd:** John Daniels 64tl; Masahiro Iijima 64br; **Corbis:** John Periam / Cordaiy Photo Library Ltd 69bc; **DK Images:** Jerry Young 70bc; **Oxford Scientific Films:** Richard Packwood 71tc; **Rex Features:** John Gooch 68–69tc; **Science Photo Library:** UCL, Grant Museum of Zoology 8–9c; FRIEDRICH SAURER 15tc; All other images © Dorling Kindersley
Illustrations by: Dan Wright

Wallchart: Alamy Stock Photo: Martin Chapman (cr/Cheetah Image). **Dreamstime.com:** Anankkml (c); Victor Lapaev (t); Holly Kuchera (cr). **naturepl.com:** Daniel Heuclin (cra). **Science Photo Library:** UCL, Grant Museum of Zoology (cla)

All other images © Dorling Kindersley.
For further information see:
www.dkimages.com